A Collins Intensive English

Compact

Elementary

SOUTHGATE COLLEGE
Faculty of Humanities
and Business Studies

Teacher's Book

Debra Powell *with*

Madeline McHugh

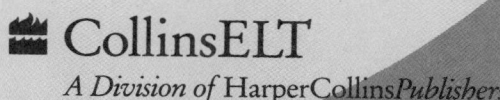

CollinsELT

A Division of HarperCollins*Publishers*

Collins ELT
HarperCollins Publishers
77-85 Fulham Palace Road
London W6 8JB

© HarperCollins Publishers Ltd. 1992

First published 1992

All rights reserved. No part of this book may be reproduced, stored in a retrieval system or transmitted in any form or by any means, electronic, mechanical, photocopying, recording or otherwise, without the prior permission in writing of the publisher.

ISBN 0 00 370501 3

Printed and bound in Great Britain by
M & A Thomson Litho Ltd, East Kilbride, Scotland.

This Teacher's Book is accompanied by a cassette ISBN 0 00 370502 1 and a Student's Book and Practice Book, ISBN 0 00 370500 5.

Contents

Introduction — v
Guiding principles • Student profile • Components • Number of teaching hours • Extending and reducing the length • Unit breakdown • Projects • Practice section • Four ways of teaching and learning • Establishing pair and group work • Presenting tasks • Presenting grammar • Presenting functions • Balance of skills • Receptive skills: reading and listening • Setting up reading and listening tasks • Productive skills: speaking and writing • Teaching pronunciation • Teaching vocabulary • Dictionary skills • Taking responsibility for learning • Helping students learn • Dealing with mistakes • Classroom management • Lesson planning

Contents and map of the Student's and Practice Book — xvi

Teacher's notes — 1
Units 1-20

Key to practice section — 41
Units 1-20

Grammar reference — 51

Tapescripts — 55
Units 1-20

Projects — 67
Project 1: Shopping chart of student's host town
Project 2: Family tree
Project 3: End of term/course party

Irregular verbs — 73

Wordlist — 74

Acknowledgements — 78

Introduction

Guiding principles

COMPACT I provides intensive, realistic and challenging study for short course students. The materials and topics are lively, stimulating and current. The coursework is based on cooperative activities where students learn from each other as well as the teacher, and listen to and contribute to an exchange of personal experiences, ideas and information. New language is taught thoroughly and revised and recycled throughout the course. *COMPACT I* also provides support and advice for the less experienced teacher.

Learning English is not merely acquiring a skill but is a wider educational process, where topical issues are investigated and discussed and students learn to take responsibility for their own learning.

Student profile

COMPACT I is designed with the following students in mind:

AGE 17+. Adults and young adults.

LEVEL OF ENGLISH. Elementary/false beginner. Students who have progressed beyond beginner level in English language learning. They have met the basic grammatical forms of English, but cannot yet use them with confidence or fluency. Students who do not yet have the active vocabulary to express complex ideas.

NATIONALITY Any nationality. Monolingual or multilingual classes. Students studying in their own country or abroad.

MOTIVATION Students with a variety of motives for learning English - for work, tourism, academic reasons, as a hobby. The topics and activities in *COMPACT I* cover a wide range of subjects to encourage classroom communication between expert and non-expert. Each can contribute more on one topic and learn from his/her neighbour on another.

CULTURE *COMPACT I* is international in approach. It assumes that students want to communicate internationally for a range of purposes. It does not assume that students' interests are limited to the life and culture of English-speaking countries.

AVAILABLE TIME Students with a limited amount of study time who want an intensive course in an enjoyable but serious context.

Components

COMPACT I Student's and Practice Book comprises: classwork section, practice section, grammar reference appendix and transcripts of the cassette material.
COMPACT I Teacher's Book comprises: comprehensive introduction to *COMPACT I* and short courses in general, teacher's notes (showing reduced pages from classwork section), key to practice section (showing reduced pages from practice section), three projects, grammar reference appendix, transcripts of the cassette materials, alphabetical wordlist with unit and exercise references, table of irregular verbs. *COMPACT I Cassette* contains all the material for the listening activities.

Number of teaching hours

The basic course length is 40-50 classroom hours in two-hour lessons. This is flexible, however, and is designed to be made shorter or longer to fit the time available. It can be reduced to approximately 20+ hours. It can be extended to 60+ hours if full use is made of the additional activities and projects. This means that students on even the shortest courses should be able to cover all twenty units and avoid the frustration of ending their course part of the way through the coursebook.

Extending and reducing the length

Exercises marked with a ⊖ symbol can be omitted without affecting the core of the course or the syllabus. Such exercises include:
- The *Vocabulary* activity and the end of every unit
- Follow-up activities which come after the *Language focus* activity
- Any reading or listening tasks related to the topic rather than the structure, which extend vocabulary rather than carry the main grammatical focus.

Exercises marked with a ⊕ symbol are additional to the core of the course and are available if students need extra practice or to extend the period of study.

INTRODUCTION

Unit breakdown

Each unit contains the following sections:
- *Saying what you think* (a speaking activity to introduce the topic)
- Main reading activity
- *Language focus* (the grammatical focus of the unit)
- Main listening activity
- Functional language
- *Vocabulary*

In addition to this, follow-up activities provide further practice of grammar and vocabulary.

One example of a typical unit:

'LANGUAGE FOCUS'
Highlights main grammatical focus of the unit. Students concentrate on accuracy.

'SAYING WHAT YOU THINK'
Speaking activity to introduce the theme of the unit. Students exchange experiences, ideas and information.

SECONDARY LISTENING
Develops vocabulary and introduces main functional point of the unit.

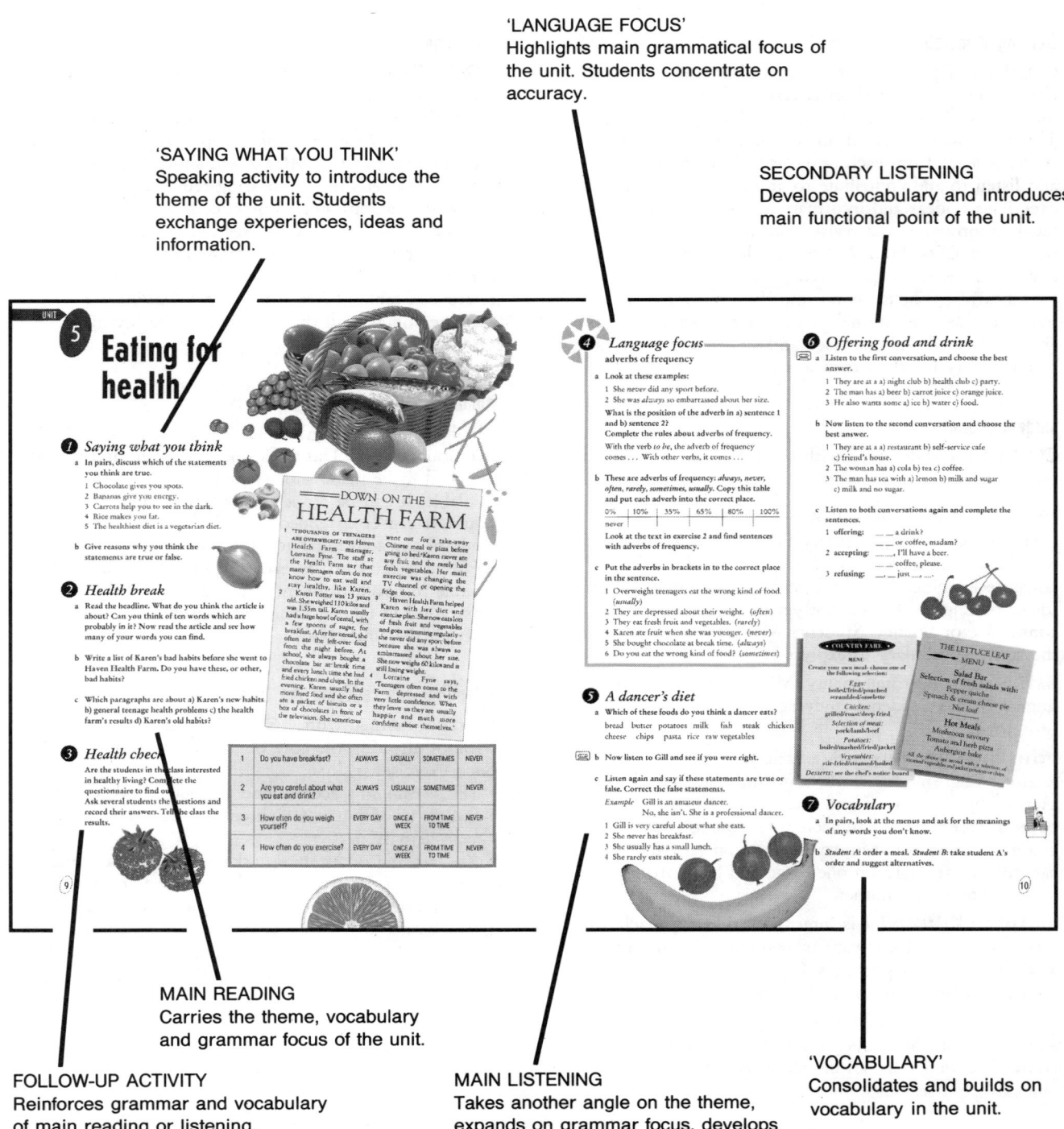

MAIN READING
Carries the theme, vocabulary and grammar focus of the unit.

FOLLOW-UP ACTIVITY
Reinforces grammar and vocabulary of main reading or listening.

MAIN LISTENING
Takes another angle on the theme, expands on grammar focus, develops vocabulary and listening strategies.

'VOCABULARY'
Consolidates and builds on vocabulary in the unit.

INTRODUCTION

The Practice Section

The **Practice Section** of *COMPACT I* is a self-study resource, designed to encourage learner independence and confidence as students complete tasks without the support and guidance of the teacher. The exercises are fully integrated with the language of the coursebook.

The exercises practice and consolidate the language presented in each unit - no new grammatical items are introduced for detailed understanding or practice. The vocabulary studied in the classwork unit is revised and extended. There are additional reading texts related to the theme of each unit. The writing exercises range from controlled patterns reinforcing the *Language focus* of the unit to tasks requiring freer communication. Material is recycled throughout the book and revision is treated as a continuous process.

Projects

COMPACT I Teacher's Book contains three projects. Project work is a student-centred activity where students make choices about, for example, what they want to say or write, the speed they work at, the amount of extra work they do, the phrases they want to use. The language learned in the formal setting of the classroom is used and practised outside in a more natural way.

Preparation is done in the helpful and secure setting of the classroom before students set off on their own.

Students are well motivated by having to decide the language they really need to use for the particular situation. These activities involve all four skills - speaking when carrying out a survey, listening to responses, writing when recording responses and writing up the results, reading when finding out more information from articles, books and notices.

1 Preparing

Discuss ideas for the project in class. Suggest ways of carrying out the project and get students to contribute their own ideas. Help clarify language students need.

2 Doing the project

Students begin organising, collecting information, conducting research and interviews for their particular project. Students should work in pairs or groups at first to build up their confidence.

3 Gathering and collating information

Students collect together all the information they have found, in groups or pairs. Students decide on the method of presentation which will best represent their work. Help with this organisational stage. Students write up their findings.

Presenting the information

Students present the results of their work to each other, for example, relaying information they have obtained, explaining and demonstrating the work they have produced.

Equipment

The equipment can be as simple as a piece of paper and pen or as sophisticated as a video camera and a computer with a desk-top publishing package. Try to assemble whatever students need in advance - for example large sheets of paper and felt-tipped pens, portable cassette players and clipboards. If there is little equipment available, get students to make themselves a folder to keep and display project work in and to keep it separate from their other coursework.

Students may be quite wary about conducting research in English with strangers. Make sure they have the appropriate language for such situations, for example: *Excuse me. Would you mind answering a few questions? I'm a student from ... and I'm preparing a guide ...* Encourage students to work in pairs or groups so that they don't feel too anxious.

You may expect students to practise a particular grammatical point in the project, for example *... is more expensive than ...* However, students may find they need to say/write something quite different. Help with any new language that is needed as well as the expected language points.

Students' enthusiasm may wane during the project, especially if they encounter any difficulties. Monitor project work regularly and always talk to each group or pair at every stage of the project to help with any problems and give further ideas and guidance.

Four ways of teaching and learning

Learning objectives can be achieved in many different ways. The four teaching and learning styles on which *COMPACT I* is based are outlined here: teacher control, pair work, group work, individual study. The detailed teaching notes for each exercise indicate which style is most appropriate.

TEACHER CONTROL Where the teacher talks to the whole class together.
- Introducing the topic
- Presenting new language items
- Eliciting short responses from students
- Drilling
- Explaining the activity
- Changing the activity at an appropriate moment
- Organising feedback from the activity
- Correcting
- Commenting on student performance
- Setting homework

PAIR AND GROUP WORK Where pupils cooperate in pairs or groups (groups will usually consist of 4 to 8 students).
- Commenting on the topic
- Practising new language
- Preparing activities
- Performing activities - listening, reading, speaking and writing
- Giving feedback to the whole class

INTRODUCTION

- Analysing texts
- Exchanging ideas in discussion
- Finding out information about each other
- Correcting each other
- Pooling knowledge

INDIVIDUAL STUDY Where students work on their own.
- Reading texts
- Listening to texts
- Preparing activities
- Taking notes
- Studying grammar references
- Writing a learner diary
- Self-correcting
- Self-testing
- Practising drills

Many of the activities can be approached in more than one way - there is not necessarily one ideal style. When correcting, for example, students can collaborate and help each other; the teacher can take full responsibility for correcting; the teacher can indicate where mistakes are for students to study and correct on their own. The teaching notes make suggestions only: choose your teaching style according to the needs of your class and your particular circumstances.

Establishing pair and group work

At the beginning of the course, you may find that some of your students are used to the teacher remaining in total control. These students may initially have a negative attitude to pair and group work. If so explain some of the
advantages:
- Extra student speaking-time
- Real conversations develop and students speak face to face
- Students take more responsibility for and can assess their own learning
- Students develop confidence in speaking without the teacher as a support, but with help available
- Extra listening practice, including a variety of accents
- Practice in listening for mistakes
- Students learn from each other
- The teacher can assess students' progress.

While students are working in pairs or groups you have an important role. Always explain the task clearly before students start the activity. Listen to pairs/groups as they are working, but don't intervene unless there is a breakdown in understanding between students. Allow them to develop their confidence and lose their inhibitions. Let them enjoy communicating their ideas and experiences without worrying unduly about accuracy. Help out if students ask for vocabulary or other language items. Take note of any students who are not participating. They might find it intimidating to be asked to speak there and then, so perhaps give them an activity to prepare at home and present to the class/group during the next lesson.

Be flexible about how long an activity goes on. Stop it before students become bored, but allow it to continue longer than planned if they are communicating well with good language pay-off. Always have a report-back activity. Give feedback yourself. Say, for example: *You did that activity very well. Now I'll just go over one or two things.*

Presenting tasks

The word 'task' is used to define any activity that students are engaged in, for example completing a form, listening to a text to answer questions, group discussion or exchanging ideas with a partner. Any combination of the four skills of speaking, listening, reading or writing may be involved. A general approach to presenting a task is outlined here:

1 Introduce the task

Explain clearly the task students have to perform. Deal with any queries students have about the task. Check their understanding - ask individual students to paraphrase the instructions or demonstrate how the task works.

2 Students perform the task

Act as a resource for students as necessary - help with difficult areas, give advice on grammar and vocabulary. Act as a prompter if necessary - help to keep things going if a discussion is flagging, for example. Make sure an activity is not dominated by one or two individuals.

3 Conduct feedback session

Students report on their answers/findings/conclusions to the class. They can comment on their own or each other's findings or ask for further explanations. Check their responses.

4 Present follow-up activity

Not every task has a follow-up activity, but there may be, for example, a homework task, an exercise from the **Practice Section**, or a group discussion around the topics raised in the text.

Presenting grammar

COMPACT I is based on two assumptions: (1) that students need to learn the grammar of English as a framework on which to build and expand; (2) that students need to practise grammar in communicative situations in order to be able to manipulate grammar effectively. Each unit of the course has a formal grammar section entitled *Language focus* which highlights the main grammar points, encouraging deductive skills and providing explanations and grammar exercise material. Learning grammar is not confined to this section however; students are also familiarising themselves with grammar whenever they listen to or read texts, exchange information and write notes, discuss ideas and give opinions.

INTRODUCTION

Students can also refer to the unit-by-unit **Grammar reference** for grammatical explanations.

USING GRAMMAR TERMS It is useful for students to learn grammatical terminology such as present simple, comparative and superlative forms of adjectives. Don't keep these names a secret - they can be used in formal or informal discussion of grammar points.

FORM AND FUNCTION Each grammatical item has a form and a function. Always teach form and function in tandem. But don't necessarily try and teach all the forms and functions that a particular item may have at once. Take care not to overload students with information.

PRESENTING NEW ITEMS Several basic procedures should be observed.
1 Present item(s) in context, e.g. a reading text.
2 Extract item(s) from context for close inspection and analysis.
3 Practise item(s) isolated in a controlled exercise, e.g. a drill.
4 Practise item(s) in a wider context in a less controlled way, e.g. getting information from your partner to complete a chart.

The grammatical presentations in *COMPACT I* encourage students to use their powers of deduction and observation, to read explanations of rules and then study examples in context and finally to implement the rules in context.

COMPARISON WITH THE MOTHER TONGUE Try not to discourage students from comparing the rules of English with those of their own language, this is an important method of analysing, understanding and learning. Students in a multilingual class can even compare how their different languages deal with a particular form/function.

DRILLS Drills and controlled practice of grammatical items will help students memorise items and build their confidence. Being able to perform a drill accurately, however, does not mean being able to use that particular form fluently. Complete accuracy cannot be expected; once students seem to have mastered a grammatical point they will probably forget it and make mistakes from time to time and need reminders and revision. There are several grammar drill books which offer further explanation and practice of isolated grammar points. Choose a book that you think will be helpful for your students and recommend it.

DEALING WITH QUERIES The *COMPACT I* syllabus includes the most appropriate grammatical points for students at elementary level. From time to time students will ask about the use or meaning of an item not included in the book. Choose a good grammar for your own reference. Never be afraid to say you don't know the answer to something. Tell students you will find out more information about their question and give an answer in the next lesson.

GRAMMAR SUMMARIES The grammatical focus of each unit is reflected in the **Grammar reference** appendix. The reference consolidates and expands on the explanations in the *Language focus* section and is intended largely for reference purposes. This provides students with a ready grammar summary as they progress through the course and after the course is over.

Presenting functions

Because functional language forms an important part of the student's repertoire of 'survival English' at the elementary level, there is a clear functional element in *COMPACT I*.

In *COMPACT I*, students hear and are asked to identify functional exponents contextualised in short listening activities. They are given an opportunity to practise these exponents and build on their knowledge of the main grammar focus of the unit in group or pairwork.

Balance of skills

COMPACT I adopts an integrated-skills approach. Because it is a short course designed for intensive study, the balance of skills is tipped towards speaking and listening. This is to maximise the opportunities for interaction and communication during the available contact hours. The course includes a wide variety of reading texts and activities, but there are deliberately fewer writing tasks. Additional writing tasks can be set as homework assignments.

Receptive skills: reading and listening

The language level of student's receptive skills (reading and listening) is usually higher than that of their productive skills (speaking and writing). Do not expect your students to be able to reproduce language accurately to the same level as they can read.

Students often find reading tasks easier than listening. A reading text will usually be grammatically accurate with a logical, step-by-step presentation of ideas or information. The written word also remains on the page to be studied at length, although many of the reading tasks may require students to skim through the text very quickly at first. Speech, on the other hand, contains other features. The spoken word does not remain static for careful study and students have to retain what they hear in their heads. Speakers change speed according to what they want to say. When students first meet listening materials they will need guidance in how to approach the task. The skills established by the format presented in *COMPACT I* will lead students to effective listening skills.

READING/LISTENING FOR GIST With both reading and listening texts encourage students to approach the whole text and not to be concerned with detailed understanding, at least the first time they read/hear it.

INTRODUCTION

Detailed analysis comes later. Encourage scanning (searching for specific pieces of information and finding them by focusing on key words) and skimming (reading for gist) - neither skill involves detailed understanding. Be prepared to repeat sections of listening texts if students are having difficulty in getting hold of the main points or ideas.

USING THE ILLUSTRATIONS Illustrations supplement the reading and listening activities. Use them e.g. to promote discussion, extend vocabulary etc.

SKILLS PRACTISED Reading and listening tasks involve the following skills:
- Predicting the ideas and information that will be presented by the writer/speaker
- Understanding the gist
- Extracting specific information
- Deducing the meaning of unknown words and phrases from their context
- Identifying patterns, such as a particular grammatical or functional usage in the text.

TASKS TO PRACTISE THE SKILLS A wide range of tasks have been designed to help students develop their reading and listening strategies:
- True/False questions
- Multiple choice questions
- Open-ended questions
- Transferring information, e.g. from text to chart
- Completing related tasks, e.g. roleplay based on a listening task, writing a short biography following a model.

Setting up reading and listening tasks

The detailed procedures for reading and listening exercises are very similar and are described together here. 'Text' here refers to both reading and listening (recorded) texts.

PREPARATION Here are some useful preparation procedures:

1 Read/Listen to the text in advance. Identify the following: problems students will meet that you need to prepare them for, suitable points in the text for pausing (mark these in the text/tapescript with an asterisk). For a listening task, check the tape recorder is in order. Set the tape counter to zero, run through the tape pausing at each asterisk marked in the tapescript and note the number on the counter. This will help you find sections in the listening material quickly during the lesson.
2 Look at the aims and objectives of the exercise and note items which need to be taught in advance.
3 Identify any appropriate revision, additional questions or language work that can be used to consolidate the learning.
4 Note any alternative teaching/learning styles you may wish to use e.g. follow-up group discussion, checking answers in pairs.

DOING THE TASK A step-by-step approach to tasks is recommended.
1 Explain the aims of the exercise to students.
2 If the students need to prepare a chart in which to record their answers, e.g. under category headings such as age, nationality, first language, they do this now.
3 Make sure that they understand the instructions.
4 Students read/listen according to the instructions.
5 Students read/listen again - this time in sections to complete/check answers.
6 Use the board to focus students' attention on important words or structures - seeing the structures isolated will help fix them in students' minds. Get students to read again/repeat important sections of the text/tape. If time allows, encourage students to make additional questions to test each other.

FOLLOW-UP This can cover a number of areas and careful preparation is recommended.
1 Consider in advance what follow-up work is appropriate - homework, project work, groupwork, pairwork and so on.
2 Give students time to discuss or note down their reaction to the exercise. Encourage them to identify any difficulties and how they could improve their performance.
3 Consider how this lesson will be related to the next one and how the vocabulary/language learned here will be revised and recycled later.

Productive skills: speaking and writing

The productive skills of speaking and writing can be improved dramatically through practice leading to greater confidence. *COMPACT I* builds up these skills in several ways.

Some tasks require students to produce short pieces of language, for example guided oral practice and writing single sentences to practise a structure. Such activities are often supported by tables which provide guidance but, at the same time, require students to make sensible choices.

For students to learn to communicate fluently in speaking/writing, they need activities where they can speak/write at length, for example exchanging information with a partner about a particular topic, finding out the opinions of the group, writing about personal experience/ideas, writing a paragraph from notes. *COMPACT I* provides plenty of such communicative tasks. Each unit opens with a speaking section, *Saying what you think*. The **Practice section** contains specific writing activities.

Throughout the course, however, skills are integrated so that the main reading and listening sections include particularly speaking, and some writing, activities, for example students comment on what they have read/listened to, they conduct surveys, write a short biography, discuss in groups their responses to the opinions presented.

ACTIVITY TYPES The speaking and writing activities in *COMPACT I* include the following:
- Asking for and giving information
- Relating personal experiences
- Describing people/places/events
- Narrating
- Presenting ideas and opinions
- Agreeing and disagreeing
- Correcting
- Social exchanges, e.g. greeting, offering, inviting

Teaching pronunciation

COMPACT I takes an integrated approach to the teaching of pronunciation - pronunciation is not seen as an isolated activity but forms an integral part of each lesson. The main aspects are:

1 Word stress

When students learn a new word they should also learn which syllable is stressed, for example:

Spanish, Chinese, Italian, Brazilian

2 Sentence stress

The words which carry the key meaning of a sentence usually have strong stress, for example:

Are you married? Angela's Italian.

Make sure students use the appropriate stress patterns for both individual words and sentences. Give them a code for marking stress, for example: ● or ' above the stressed syllable. Occasionally ask students to listen to three or four lines of dialogue from a listening text, write down what is said and mark it with the stress indicators.

3 Weak forms

Just as some words and syllables are given strong stress, others are given very weak stress, for example:

I've got two brothers and three sisters.

The frequency of weak stress is usually greater than that of strong stress.

The most common weak stress in English occurs in the sound shown by the phonetic symbol /ə/. This sound is called 'schwa' and it appears several times in most sentences. It is the vowel sound found in *the* when the following word begins with a consonant (as in: *the pen*). The following examples give some indication of the frequency of 'schwa' in sentences. Letters in bold print denote the occurrence of 'schwa':
*Where **a**re you going **a**t the weekend? - To the theatre.*
*She wants to walk the length **o**f Afric**a**.*
Encourage students to listen for and mark letters and syllables which carry this sound.

4 Rhythm

The pattern of weak and strong sounds makes a particular rhythm. Look at these rhythmic patterns and the example sentences for each one:

Where does she live? ●●●●
What about you? ●●●●
Peaches and cream. ●●●●
Her mother's Italian. ●●●●●
I can't understand it. ●●●●●
Is France far from Denmark? ●●●●●●

Get students to recognise rhythm patterns by, for example, clapping/beating the rhythm of sentences, marking rhythmic sound patterns as above, composing different sentences to fit a particular rhythmic pattern.

5 Intonation

Intonation is the way the voice rises and falls in sentences and a very important part of meaning. It can indicate, for example, surprise, interest, lack of interest, disbelief, politeness or rudeness. If students are unaware of intonation in English, they can be seriously misunderstood.

Try saying the word *No* with four different intonation patterns to register (1) surprise (2) anger (3) uncertainty (4) disbelief and notice how your intonation changes radically each time.

Make sure students practise the correct intonation when they are learning new phrases:

Would you like tea or coffee?
I'm afraid I don't know.
What's the matter?

From time to time, get students to mark intonation patterns in sentences in this way.

6 Problem sounds

Some sounds in English are a particular problem for speakers of a certain language. Differentiating between these words, for example:
jot and *yacht* - Spanish speakers
live and *leave* - Italian speakers
chick and *tick* - Portuguese speakers
think and *sink* - French speakers
If you come across this problem, write a few examples on the board of words which show the problem sounds. Say one of the words, and get students to indicate which one you are saying. Don't spend a great deal of time on this activity and don't ask students to repeat the sounds more than a couple of times.

7 Linkage

In spoken English the end of one word often merges into the beginning of the next. This is not lazy or sloppy speech but correct pronunciation. Look at what happens to the *t* sound between *want* and *to* in this sentence:

I want‿to go there.

The two *t* sounds merge. Sometimes linkage between words is helped by the addition of small sounds, for example:

Have you⁽ʷ⁾ever been to⁽ʷ⁾India?

INTRODUCTION

Show me in a minute.

Teach students how to make these linkages if they are having difficulty in pronouncing sentences fluently. Write examples of the small linking sounds on the board.

Many students do not want perfect English pronunciation and do not want to be mistaken for native English speakers or lose their identity as, for example, native Spanish or Chinese speakers. The aim of guidance on pronunciation is to enable students to understand spoken English more easily and to be more easily understood themselves. Don't overdo pronunciation. Never allow students to ridicule the pronunciation of others in the class.

Teaching vocabulary

It is particularly important for elementary level students to develop strategies for understanding or dealing with new vocabulary. For this reason, the last section in every unit of *COMPACT I* contains a vocabulary extension activity.

The vocabulary in section 6 or 7 is always related to the topic of the unit, though it may be either new vocabulary or vocabulary which has already been introduced in the unit and is being reinforced.
The activities in this section are interesting and challenging. Though students are, of course, encouraged to use their dictionaries to find the meanings of the vocabulary items in this section, in many cases they should be able to work out the meaning of the items from the context.
COMPACT I encourages students to develop their vocabulary learning skills using, for example:
• Word families
• Thematic words
• Synonyms
• Cloze texts
• Grouping words of similar type
• Matching words and illustrations
• Understanding signs and symbols
• Matching words and definitions
• Understanding abbreviations.

Dictionary skills

Students should learn to use their dictionaries during classwork and when working on their own. Any dictionary work in *COMPACT I* relates to the *Collins Cobuild English Language Dictionary* (see the introduction to this dictionary for further information and ideas for use). Make clear to students that a good dictionary is not only a translation tool but a means of increasing their knowledge of all aspects of the language. Spend some time at the beginning of the course familiarising the students with the conventions of a dictionary - the format of the entries, the signs and symbols used and the reference skills and insights into the language that students can gain by using their dictionaries properly.

The *Collins Cobuild English Language Dictionary* gives the following information:
• Meaning and use
• Spelling
• Stress
• Pronunciation
• Word families, e.g. synonyms and prefixes
• Grammar, e.g. prepositions used with adjectives
• Idiomatic use
• Dialect forms, e.g. British and American English.

Taking responsibility for learning

COMPACT I aims to give students the language and skills they need to take control of their own learning - what they learn, how much and how quickly. Students often feel they have to depend on the teacher to tell them what to do and how to do it. Point out right at the beginning what procedures they can adopt to augment the learning that takes place in a formal class setting - either at home to supplement homework or even in the classroom, for example when they are waiting for others to finish. Here are some ways to improve individual learning:

1 Realistic repetition

With a partner, students can roleplay short dialogues. Working alone they can envisage a situation and practise the language in their heads, for example:

I passed!
Oh, well done! Congratulations!
Thanks!

2 Substitution drills

Students can produce their own drill by taking a structure and repeating it with substitutions - perhaps the person, the time, the location, the frequency, for example:

He walks to work every day.
We walk to work every day.
They walk to school every day.
They walk to school on Mondays.

3 Written language

Written forms can aid students' memory so students should use reading and writing to help. Students can note down new material - remember new language lexis or structures - in their books in this way:

amateur
Amateur
Gill is an amateur dancer.

4 Self-testing

Students should not feel that they have to wait for the teacher to test their language. Show them how to write new lexis and structures in their exercise books with the coursebook closed and check for errors. Working in pairs they can test each other.

5 Jumbled words and structures

Students can make up short tests for each other by taking a word or structure and mixing up the letters or the words and seeing if they can put it back together again, for example:

clnciee - licence

must clean licence have driving a you.
You must have a clean driving licence.

6 Classroom language

For maximum benefit from classwork, students need to be able to use and respond to the language that they encounter in the classroom. Make sure students use English to ask for further explanation or repetition, for example:

How do you spell ...?
What does ... mean?
How do you say ... in English?
What's the meaning of ...?

7 Learning after the course

If students develop strategies for learning during the course, they will be well-equipped to continue learning independently after the course is over. Other learning tips which students might find useful for after the course are:

- Practise expressions silently while, e.g. waiting at a bus stop, sitting on a train
- Keep a course folder and diary for future reference
- Buy an English language newspaper once a month
- Listen to radio or TV programmes in English
- Read graded readers
- Keep a vocabulary notebook.

Helping students learn

Encouragement and achievement are the food and drink of the language learner. Students have differing abilities and learn at different rates - it is important to take this into consideration and encourage and praise the individual as well as the whole class. Where a student is struggling, identify the problem and suggest ways that the student can proceed with his/her learning.

Students keep a daily diary of what they learn, which might have these headings:

DATE

GRAMMAR STUDIED

USEFUL PHRASES

USEFUL VOCABULARY

PROBLEMS

BOOK PAGE REFERENCE

Dealing with mistakes

Three important points about mistakes:

1 Making mistakes is part of the learning process.
2 Mistakes tell the teacher what the students do not know.
3 Students can often correct themselves and correct each other.

Correcting mistakes

- If you correct every single mistake, you will inhibit students' desire to communicate.
- Students often make mistakes because they have temporarily forgotten something - all they need is a gentle reminder.
- If a group of students makes the same mistake on a point they have just been taught, they need revision as a group.
- Students may make mistakes because they do not know the correct way of expressing something - they need to be taught.
- When students are trying to communicate fluently don't intervene with corrections. Make a note of important mistakes and during the feedback session, ask if anyone can say this more accurately. Mistakes often mean students are experimenting and rule-testing; this is an essential part of learning and not to be discouraged. Never allow anyone to ridicule another student for his/her mistakes.

MISTAKES IN WRITTEN WORK All the above points apply here also.

- Encourage students to check their work carefully before handing it in.
- Write examples of sentences containing mistakes on the board, and get the class to correct them.
- Produce a sample piece of writing including many of the common errors which students in the group have made. Photocopy it and get students to correct it.

A marking strategy

There are several possible strategies:

- Underline important mistakes and get students to self-correct.
- Develop a system of margin notes to indicate what type of mistake a student has made, e.g. *Sp* = spelling mistake, *WO* = incorrect word order. Students correct their work themselves or in pairs.
- Indicate the number of mistakes in one paragraph and get students to find and correct their own mistakes.
- Never cover a page of work in red ink - this is very discouraging.
- Choose carefully which mistakes to ignore and which to correct. Correct any mistakes you think will seriously impede comprehension. You may sometimes have to re-phrase students' sentences to show them a clearer or more idiomatic way of expressing their information/ideas.
- Write comments on students' work to show you have read and understood what they are saying, e.g. *That sounds like a very unusual experience.* Write positive

INTRODUCTION

comments to encourage students where appropriate, e.g. *Your work is really improving*.

Classroom management

A few simple rules can help lessons run smoothly. Execute your plans efficiently, respond to students' queries and have the same rules for everyone - including yourself.

- Establish a code of conduct right from the start and keep to it, for example "Be punctual" and "Hand in homework on time".
- Prepare lessons. Outline the lesson objectives to students and allow a few moments at the end to discuss whether they have been achieved. Be flexible about lesson planning and respond to the mood of the class - allow more time for a popular activity and cut short a less successful one.
- Prepare and check all equipment in advance, for example markers and chalk, a working cassette player, enough copies of books/worksheets.
- Get students to arrange the classroom furniture quickly at the beginning of the lesson. Different arrangements suit different lessons so decide on this beforehand. Avoid moving the furniture about too much during the lesson.
- Get to know students' names quickly. Write a class plan until you know everyone. Make sure students know each other's names.
- Never be afraid to ask other teachers for ideas or advice. All teachers have met problems with individual students or groups of students. Often their advice can be very helpful.

Lesson planning

It is helpful to prepare a detailed lesson plan for each lesson.

Keep all your lesson plans for future reference. You will find a suggested lesson plan on the following page.

Lesson Plan

Date: _____
Class: _____ Time: _____
Length of lesson: _____ Number: _____
Item: _____
_____
_____
_____
_____
_____

Skills: _____
_____
_____
_____

Books: _____
Unit: _____
Exercise: _____
Page: _____
Homework: _____
_____
_____

What achieved: _____
_____
_____
_____

Problems: _____
_____
_____
_____

Comments: _____
_____
_____
_____

Contents and Map of the Book

SS = Student's Section   PS = Practice Section
GR = Grammar Reference   TS = Tapescripts

UNIT	TOPICS	STRUCTURES	FUNCTIONS/SITUATIONS
1 Make a date! SS page 1 PS page 41 GR page 61 TS page 65	meeting people	present simple questions; short answers	greetings and leave taking, formal and informal; asking for and giving personal information
2 Home and family SS page 3 PS page 42 GR page 61 TS page 66	home and family	*have got*; *what ... like?*; present simple	talking about families and homes
3 Fancy that! SS page 5 PS page 43 GR page 61 TS page 66	ambitions	present continuous; *want + to +* infinitive	describing ambitions; requesting information; making appointments over the phone
4 Detective work SS page 7 PS page 44 GR page 61 TS page 67	crime and mystery	past simple, affirmative and question forms with *to be* and other verbs	describing past events; discussing possibilities
5 Eating for health SS page 9 PS page 45 GR page 61 TS page 67	health and diet	adverbs of frequency	describing habits; offering, accepting and refusing food
6 What a job! SS page 11 PS page 46 GR page 62 TS page 68	people at work	*love, like, enjoy +* gerund; *too* and *very +* adjective	describing activities you like and dislike; asking for meaning; talking about jobs
7 You can do it! SS page 13 PS page 47 GR page 62 TS page 69	ways of communicating	*can/could* for ability	talking about languages; making and disagreeing with suggestions
8 Twenties' fever SS page 15 PS page 48 GR page 62 TS page 69	life in the 1920s	past simple, negatives and question forms	asking questions and giving information about past events
9 Are you green? SS page 17 PS page 49 GR page 62 TS page 69	environment and conservation	imperative in affirmative and negative forms	giving and following directions; asking for and giving opinions; agreeing and disagreeing
10 Leisure time SS page 19 PS page 50 GR page 62 TS page 70	leisure	present continuous for future arrangements	making, accepting and refusing invitations

UNIT	TOPICS	STRUCTURES	FUNCTIONS/SITUATIONS
11 My own business SS page 21 PS page 57 GR page 62 TS page 71	business and enterprise	*how much, how many*; tense revision	giving news; sympathising and congratulating
12 Marriage SS page 23 PS page 52 GR page 63 TS page 72	marriage	*going to* + infinitive for future plans	giving opinions; agreeing and disagreeing
13 Tips for travellers SS page 25 PS page 53 GR page 63 TS page 72	travel	modals: *must, should* and *can*	giving advice; dealing with money
14 Whizz kids SS page 27 PS page 54 GR page 63 TS page 73	genuises	present perfect simple	checking understanding
15 Two's company SS page 29 PS page 55 GR page 63 TS page 74	twins	comparatives and superlatives	making comparisons
16 What next? SS page 31 PS page 56 GR page 63 TS page 74	the future	*will* and *might* for future certainty and possibility	making predictions; expressing hopes
17 A sense of adventure SS page 33 PS page 57 GR page 64 TS page 74	holidays	countable and uncountable nouns; *there is/are* + quantifiers	making complaints and apologies
18 Golden years SS page 35 PS page 58 GR page 64 TS page 75	old age	present perfect simple with *for* and *since*	offering, accepting and refusing help; talking about experiences
19 Fun and games SS page 37 PS page 59 GR page 64 TS page 76	games	*must, have to* and negative forms *must not, don't have to*	describing rules; persuading and conceding
20 Animal facts SS page 39 PS page 60 GR page 64 TS page 76	animals	first conditional, *will* and *won't*	expressing fears and dislikes

TEACHER'S NOTES

Unit 1
Make a date!

> **Aims**
> **Structures:** Present simple tense in questions, short answers
> **Functions:** Greetings and leavetaking, formal and informal, asking for and giving personal information
> **Lexis:** expressions, Cheerio!, strangers, colleague, personal, agency, ideal, surname, first name, address, sex, nationality, Brazilian, occupation, marital status, interests, personality, fashionable, French, English, travel, small ads, classical, pop (music), squash, discos, cinema, photo, relationship

S **① Saying what you think**
Ways of greeting and saying goodbye.

a • Discuss who the people in the pictures might be. Students decide whether they are saying hello or goodbye.
  • Focus on appropriate ways of greeting and saying goodbye in these situations.

b • Write students' answers and suggestions on the board under the headings *meeting people* and *leaving people*.

Answer key
Meeting people: Good morning. Hello Hi! How are you? How do you do? Pleased to meet you.
Leaving people: Bye. Cheerio! Goodbye. Good night. See you later. See you soon.

L·S **② Personal information**
Listening for personal information and form-filling.

a • Go through the form with students, pre-teaching vocabulary. Make sure students understand the concept of 'ideal friend', ie the best possible friend.
  • Students ask and answer questions about Renato and his ideal friend: eg What's his surname? Where does he live? What about his ideal friend?

b, c • Students copy the headings from the form in their notebooks before they listen.
  • Students listen to the tape to note Josette's personal details under the headings and describe her.

Answer key
Josette - *Surname:* Aparis, *Sex:* female, *Nationality:* French, *Occupation:* student, *Interests:* travel, music (all kinds), *Personality:* serious, not shy, *Smoker:* yes

Josette would not be a good friend for Renato because: she smokes, and she speaks English better than he.
⊕ • Students compare answers with 2a, between playings of the tape.

③ Language focus
Present simple tense in questions.

a • Students read through the examples and in pairs, make similar questions, using the cues.
  • Write their suggestions on the board.

Answer key
What's your address? Are you married? Are you interested in (the theatre)? How tall are you? Do you smoke?

b • Elicit examples of questions taking these answers from students and write them on the board.
  • Put students in pairs to write 5 more questions each for the answers Yes, I am/No, I'm not. Yes, I do/No, I don't.
  • Students ask and answer their questions in pairs.

Answer key
Questions which can take, 'Yes I am./ No, I'm not.': Are you interested in...?, Are you married?
Questions which can take, 'Yes, I do./ No, I don't.': Do you smoke?
⊕ • Students tell the class about their partner.

W·S **④ Ideal friends** ⊖
Interview and form-filling activity.

a • Students copy headings from the form from exercise 2 in their notebooks before working in pairs.

b • To choose their ideal friend, students exchange their forms with other members of the group.
⊕ • Students tell the class what their partner's ideal friend is like.

R·W **⑤ Small ads** ⊖
Reading and matching exercise based on photographs, small ads, and letter extracts.

a • Students individually match the ads with the photographs.
  • Students compare answers in pairs and then give reasons for their choices.

Answer key
Ad 1 - photo B, **Ad 2** - photos A + C, **Ad 3** - photo D

b • Students, individually or in pairs, match the ads with the letters and give reasons for the matches they have made.

Answer key
Ad 1 - letter 2, **Ad 2** - letter 1

TEACHER'S NOTES

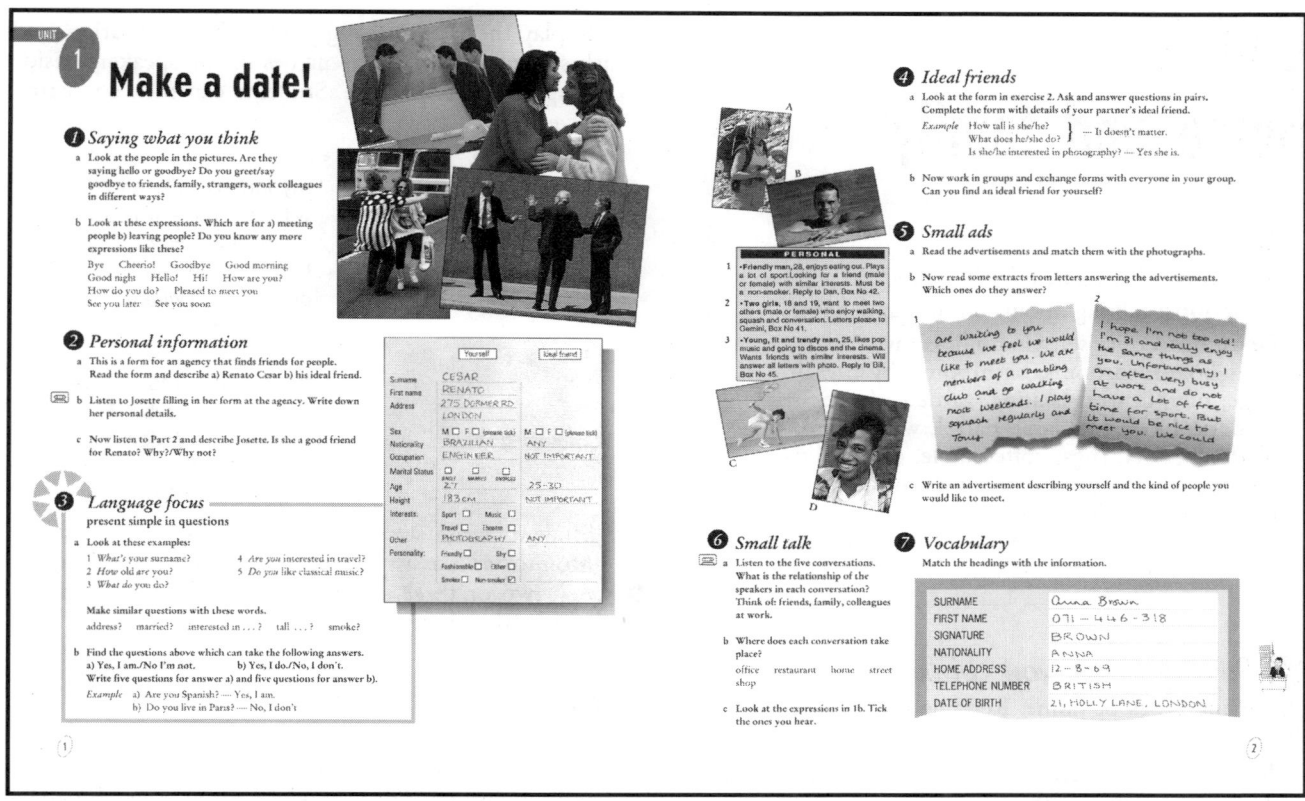

⊕ • Students exchange advertisements and write short letters of reply.

L ⑥ *Small talk*

Listening to five short conversations and identifying the relationship between the speakers and where they are.

a • Pause the tape after each conversation and ask students what they think the relationship of the speakers is.
• Record students' responses on the board, under the headings *Friend*, *Colleague*, *Family*.

b • Replay the tape, pausing after each conversation for students to take notes about where the speakers are.
• Students discuss their answers in pairs.

Answer key

Relationship	Location
A friends	on the street
B colleagues	business meeting
C friends, family	boy introducing new friend to family
D colleagues	colleagues greeting one another at the office
E friends	saying goodbye after a meal together

c • Ask students if they remember hearing any of the expressions in 1b. Play the tape for them to check their answers.

⊕ • In pairs, students write a short dialogue which they read aloud to the class. The rest of the class guess the relationship of the speakers and where they are.

W ⑦ *Vocabulary* ⊖

Matching exercise.

• Students work individually and check their answers in pairs.

Answer key

Surname: Brown, *First name:* Anna, *Signature:* Anna Brown, *Nationality:* British, *Home address:* 21 Holly Lane, London, *Telephone number:* 071 446 318, *Date of birth:* 12/8/69

Extension activity

A letter of introduction

Write a short letter introducing yourself to the class. Talk about your surname, nationality, interests etc. Students write similar letters of introduction to you.

TEACHER'S NOTES

Unit 2
Home and family

Aims
Structures: *have got, what's ... like?*
Functions: talking about families and homes.
Lexis: home, house, windmill, caravan, flat, houseboat, bedrooms, bathrooms, by myself, huge, tiny, central heating, garden, electricity, modern, block (of flats), barrel, whisky vat, platform, sofa, rugs, coffee table, circles, boxes, interior designer, plan, radiators, fitted wardrobes, reading lamp, (chest of) drawers, thirties, family tree, grandfather/mother, nephew, niece, cousin

S ❶ *Saying what you think*
Discussing types of home. Revising questions in the simple present tense.

- Elicit names of different types of home and write up student suggestions on the board.

a • Students match the homes with the photographs and answer the questions.
• Check students' pronunciation of compound nouns: windmill, caravan, houseboat.

Answer key
photos from left to right: windmill, houseboat, house, flat
house - photo 2, **windmill** - photo 4, **flat** - photo 3, **houseboat** - photo 1

b • Get students to ask you the questions first.
• Students work together asking and answering questions.
- Students write 2 more questions to ask their partner.
• Students report back to the class about their partner.

L·S ❷ *A home of my own*
Listening to three people describing their homes and matching each speaker with the correct photo from exercise 1.

a • Pause the tape after each conversation and give students a chance to match the speaker with the photograph. Students should give you reasons for their choices.

Answer key
a **Willem** - windmill, **Hiro** - flat, **Florence** - house

b • Make sure that students know the names of the 3 speakers: Willem, Hiro and Florence.

• Replay the tape, pausing after each conversation, and ask students to write the names of the speakers beside the appropriate sentence. Students can then compare answers.

Answer key
b I live with	my family. - Florence
	with friends. - Willem
	by myself. - Hiro
My home is	huge. - Florence.
	quite big. - Willem
	tiny. - Hiro
It has got	one room. - Hiro
	three bedrooms. - Willem
	three bathrooms. - Florence
It hasn't got	electricity. - Willem
	central heating. - Willem
	a garden. - Hiro

c • Students write statements individually.
• Monitor and assist students while they're writing.
- Ask two or three students to read their statements aloud to the class.

❸ *Language focus*
Have got.

a • Introduce have got by telling students about your family, house etc. Write model sentences on the board.
• Students read the examples.

b • Students complete the sentences and then compare answers with a partner.

Answer key
b 1 has got 2 have ('ve) got 3 Have...got 4 have got ... have got 5 have...got, have...got

what ... like?

a • Look at the example with the students.
• Put prompts on the board: town, home, sister, mother, job, best friend etc. and get students to ask you questions using: What ... like? Ask the students similar questions.

b • Students work together asking and aswering questions using the prompts on the board.
- Students tell the class what they have found out about their partner.

R·W ❹ *Home in a barrel*
Reading a short text about an unusual home and taking notes.

a • Pre-teach key vocabulary, before students read and answer the questions.

Answer key
a 1 He's a professor. 2 In a barrel. 3 Comfortable.

b • Students prepare lists in pairs or individually and then compare their answers with a partner.

Teacher's Notes

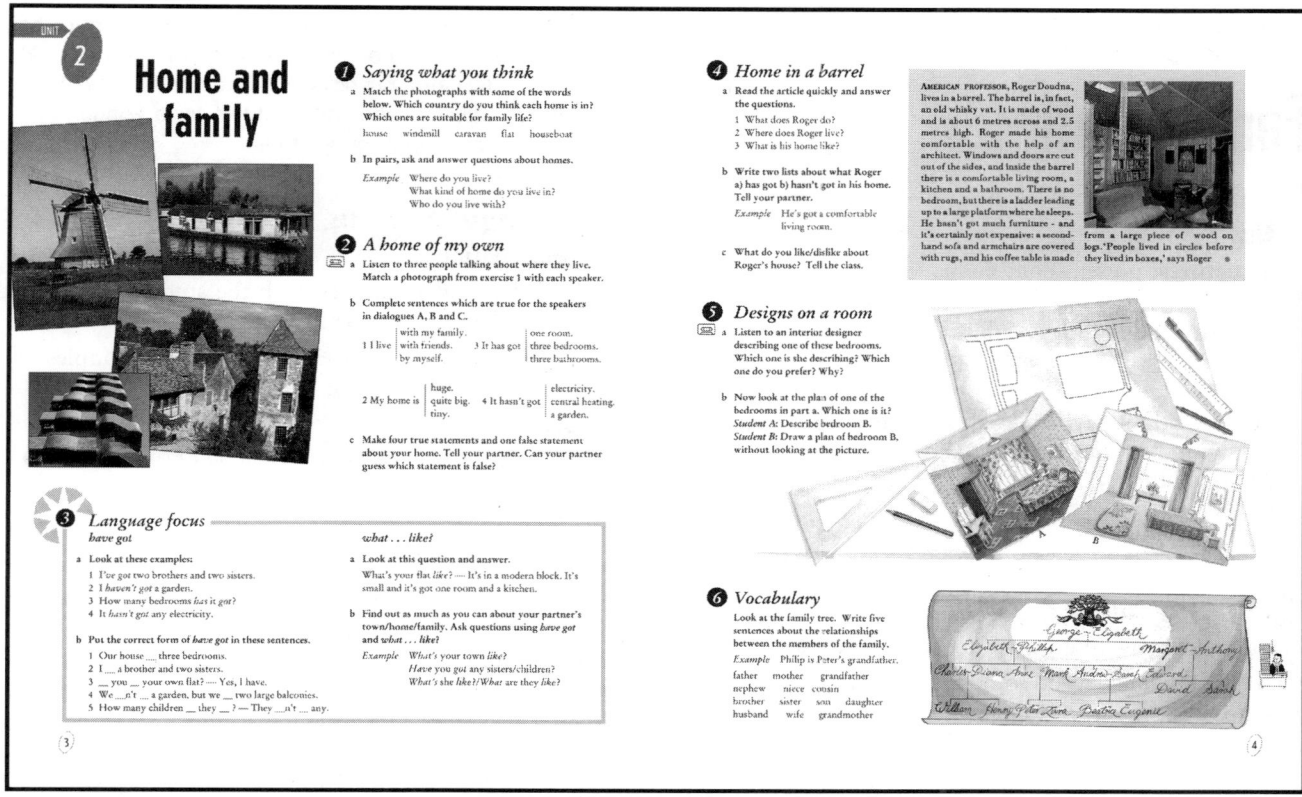

- Students make lists and then tell the class what they have/haven't got in their own homes.

Answer key
Roger has got: a comfortable living room, a kitchen, a bathroom, a large platform where he sleeps, a sofa and armchairs, rugs, a coffee table.
Roger hasn't got: a bedroom, a lot of furniture/expensive furniture.

- c • Students discuss what they like and dislike about the homes in exercise 1.

L·S ⑤ Designs on a room
Listening to a description of a bedroom and matching it with the correct picture. Describing rooms and drawing plans.

a • Elicit or pre-teach key vocabulary. Students describe the 3 bedrooms briefly. Students listen and decide which of the three bedrooms the interior designer is describing, giving reasons for their choice.

Answer key
Room B

b • Help students who are stuck. Note errors while students are working in pairs but don't correct until the end of the activity.
- Students describe a room in their own home and their partner draws a plan.

⑥ Vocabulary
Describing family relationships.

a • Draw your own family tree on the board and pre-teach the vocabulary.

Answer key
a They are the British royal family and they live in Great Britain.

b • Ask students questions like: Who is George? Who is George's wife?
- Students ask one another in open pairs around the classroom.

Extension activities

1 Floorplan:
Students do a floorplan for a room in their own home and label the rooms and the furniture.

2 Profile:
Students write a profile of their partner's town, home or family, using the information they gathered in the Language focus section b, *what ... like?*. Ensure they use "have got".

TEACHER'S NOTES

Unit 3
Fancy that!

Aims
Structures: present continuous tense; want + to + infinitive
Functions: describing ambitions, requesting information, making appointments over the phone
Lexis: work, study, health, travel, marriage, preparations, journey, want(s), the length of, distance, dream, collecting, drivers, advice, factory, marathon, pass (a test), book (a lesson)

S ❶ Saying what you think
Asking and answering questions about ambitions.
a • To help students, write some future ambitions on the board, under the headings *I want to.../I don't want to*.
b • To introduce the activity, students can ask you the questions.
⊕ • One or two students tell the class about their partner's ambitions.

R ❷ African walk
Reading a short text and answering comprehension questions.
⊕ a • Before reading, bring in a map of Africa and get students to guess 1) the length in km and 2) how long it would take to walk across it at a rate of 40km per day.
• Students read the text through once quickly for the answers to questions 1 and 2.
Answer key
1 She wants to walk the length of Africa. 2 She is collecting money for the walk.
b • Students read the text again and discuss the answers to questions 1-3 in groups.
⊕ • Students underline 5 words they would like to know the meaning of and ask other students and the teacher.
Answer key
1 She is looking for two drivers, fitting the car with beds and a shower, buying things she needs for the trip, and collecting money.
2 *14,000 km* - the distance Ffyona wants to walk, *13* - Ffyona plans to spend *13* months on the journey, *40* - she plans to walk *40* km per day, *16* - she was *16* when she walked the length of Britain, *18* - when she was *18* years old, she walked across the U.S.A.,

£50,000 - the amount of money she has collected for her African trip, *30* - she needs *30* pairs of training shoes, *60* - she needs *60* pairs of socks, *50* - she needs *50* bottles of shampoo, *£25,000* - she collected this for a London hospital on her trip through Britain.

❸ Language focus
Present continuous.
a • Read the model sentence with the students and elicit that 'is collecting' means a) 'now'.
b • Students underline or note down other examples of the present continuous in the text.
Answer key
is planning, is writing, is collecting, is looking, is fitting, is buying

Want + to + infinitive.
a • Students read the model sentence aloud and find other examples in the text. Write these up on the board.
Answer key
a 1 She *wants to walk* the length of Africa... 2 She *wants to be* comfortable after each day's walk... 3 On her African expedition, she *wants to collect* much more money... 4 ... 'If *you really want to do* something...'
b • Students complete the sentences individually.
Answer key
1 ... is looking for... 2 ...wants to find... 3 ... is writing...
4 ... do you want to complete...? 5 ...are you doing...?
6 ...am preparing ... am collecting...

L ❹ Dreams come true ⊖
Listening to a radio phone-in programme and answering questions.
a • Preteach key vocabulary. Students read the questions. Play the tape in sections, pausing after each person phones in. Students can discuss their answers in pairs between playings of the tape.
Answer key
a 1 Three people phone in. 2 Sue wants to go to Hong Kong. Alan wants to run in the New York Marathon. Matthew wants to pass his driving test. 3 Sue is working in a factory and saving money. Alan is running 20 miles a day and watching his diet. Matthew is having driving lessons every day.
b • Ask students to answer the true/false questions from memory before you replay the tape.
• Play the tape for students to check their answers.
Answer key
b 1 false 2 true 3 false 4 false 5 true 6 false

TEACHER'S NOTES

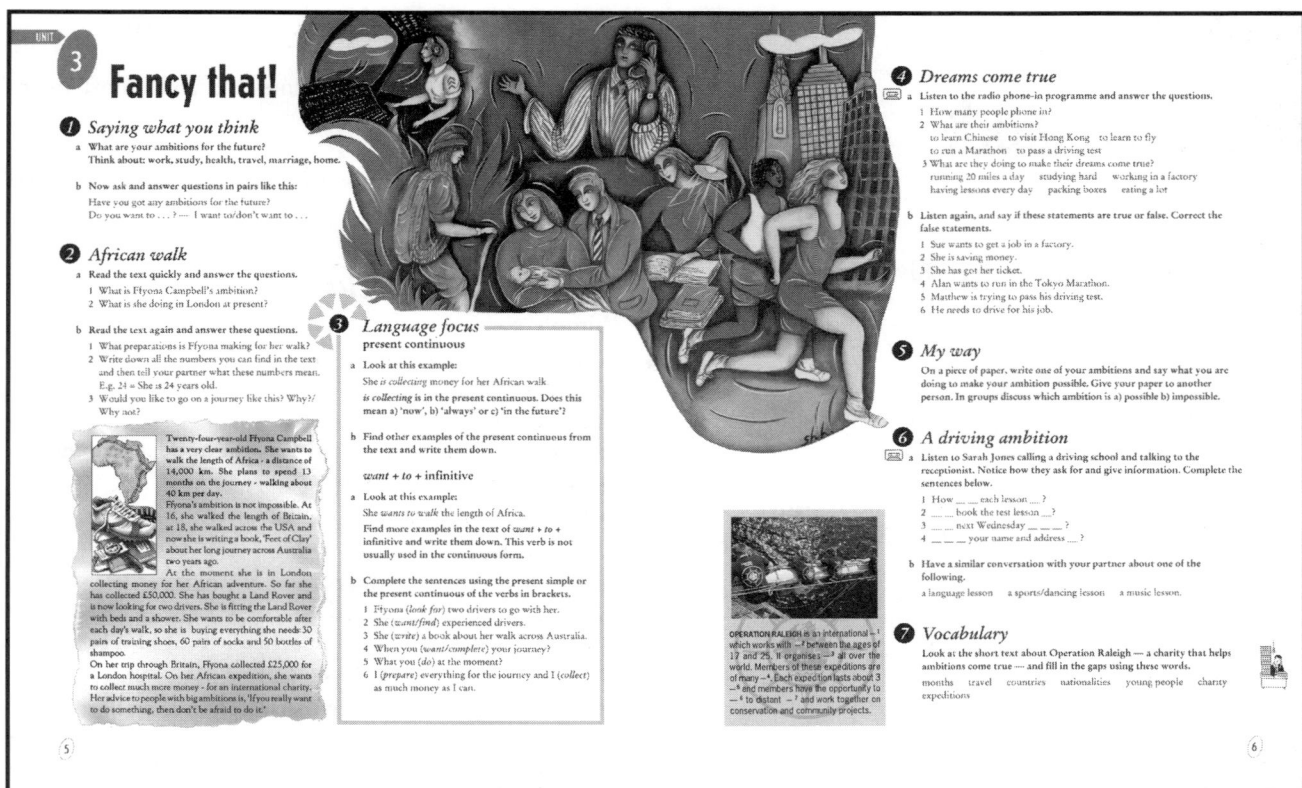

S·W ⑤ My way ⊖

Writing about and discussing ambitions as a group.

- Remind students of the headings in exercise 1 a.
- Give students an example of one of your ambitions and what you are doing to make it possible.
- Students write about their ambitions. Help students as necessary while they are writing.
- Explain the terms *possible* and *impossible*. Students then discuss in groups.
- Appoint a group secretary/spokesperson to take notes. The spokesperson should report to the class what the ambitions of the members were and the group reactions to them.
- ⊕ Read the ambitions of an internationally famous person to the class (these can be made-up) and students guess which person you are talking about.

L·S ⑥ A driving ambition

Listening to a dialogue as preparation for a roleplay.

a • Play the tape through several times, pausing for students to repeat key phrases and complete the sentences.

Answer key
1 ... much does... cost?   2 Could I ... please?   3 How about ... at four o'clock?   4 Could I have ... please?

b • Provide Students A and B (in pairs) with the following information: **SA** 1 music/language/sports lesson   2 ... how much...?   3 ... one lesson please?   4 ... That's fine/That's o.k.   5 Mr/Ms ... 12 Acorn Drive   6 Thanks...
SB 1 ... of course...   2 ... £4.50 for one lesson.   3 ... Yes. ... Tuesday at 6 o'clock?   4 ... name and address...?
- Inform the pairs that Student A begins the dialogue. You may wish to write the first two lines on the board.
- Students rehearse their roleplay.
- One or two pairs perform their roleplay in front of the class.
- ⊕ Students write the conversation.

⑦ Vocabulary ⊖

Gap-fill activity.

- Students fill in the gaps and discuss the vocabulary.
- ⊕ Students write a paragraph about a charity that they know.

Extension activity
Survey
In groups, students write three questions about ambitions in an area of their choice, eg work, travel, etc. They put their questions to other members of their group and present their results to the class.

TEACHER'S NOTES

Unit 4
Detective work

Aims
Structures: past simple, affirmative and question forms with *to be* and other verbs
Functions: describing past events, discussing possibilities
Lexis: detective, intelligent, quick-thinking, energetic, politics, science, retired, spy, active, famous, government, bees, philosophy, politics, literature, solved, case(s), assistant, country, habits, arrested, explanation, solution, released, veil, gloves, pale, throat, (to) get on/off, old-fashioned, compartment, protesting, dead, disappeared, finger, garden, murder, prison, strangle, punishment, poisonous, berries, pick-pocket(s), burglar, kidnapped, hijack, vandalism

S **1** *Saying what you think*
Discussing famous fictional detectives.

a • Students identify the detectives in the photos.
• Ask students if they read detective stories or watch detective programmes on television.
⊕ • Students tell you who wrote about the detectives.

Answer key
Sherlock Holmes, Hercule Poirot, Columbo, Miss Marple

b • Make sure that students understand the meaning of the words. They will need to use their dictionaries and discuss with the class/teacher.
• Students discuss the qualities they think a detective needs to have.

R·L **2** *Elementary, my dear Watson!*
Reading about and listening to the life of Sherlock Holmes.

⊕ • Ensure students know that Sherlock Holmes is a fictional character. Ask if they have read any books about him.

a • Students read the text and select the correct answers.

Answer key
1 b   2 b   3 b

b • Play the first part of the cassette. Students tell you who is being interviewed (Alison Thomas) and why (she has just written a book about Sherlock Holmes).
• Play the rest of the tape. Students complete the sentences.

• Students compare answers. Replay the tape, if necessary.
• Students discuss what Holmes did and report their conclusions to the class.

Answer key
1 ... got tired ... wanted   2 he continued ... work   3 ... got married ... retired.

3 *Language focus*
Simple past.

⊕ a • Write 3 or 4 example sentences from your own life on the board: *I was born in ... , I studied ... at ...*, and ask students to identify the verb.
• Students identify the verbs in the model sentences about Sherlock Holmes.

b • Students find the verbs in the text.

Answer key
was born   went   studied   was   knew   left   started   became   solved   shared   got married   moved out   continued   married   retired   kept   studied   did ... retire   became

c • Students work together to complete the chart.
• Students take it in turns to tell the story of Sherlock Holmes, one student taking up the story where another has left off.

Answer key
... was born ... went ... was ... a lot about philosophy ...left ...work as a detective ... his assistant, Dr John Watson... shared ... got married... ... to help Holmes... ... to the country... ...was...

⊕ • Students write 3 questions to ask a partner about his/her life.
⊕ • Students tell their life story.

R·S·L **4** *The Woman in Black* ⊖
Rearranging a jumbled text. Asking questions to find the solution to a mystery and then listening for the answer.

a,b • Give the best student in each group the tapescript to read while the others in the group order the text and prepare their questions.
• Make sure students know they can only ask questions requiring a 'Yes/No/I don't know' answer. In groups, students question the student who has read the tapescript.
• Students tell the class what solution, if any, they have decided upon.

c • Play the tape for students to listen for the solution.
⊕ • In pairs, students take turns telling the story.
⊕ • Students write a summary of the story.

Answer key
3, 2, 4, 1

Teacher's Notes

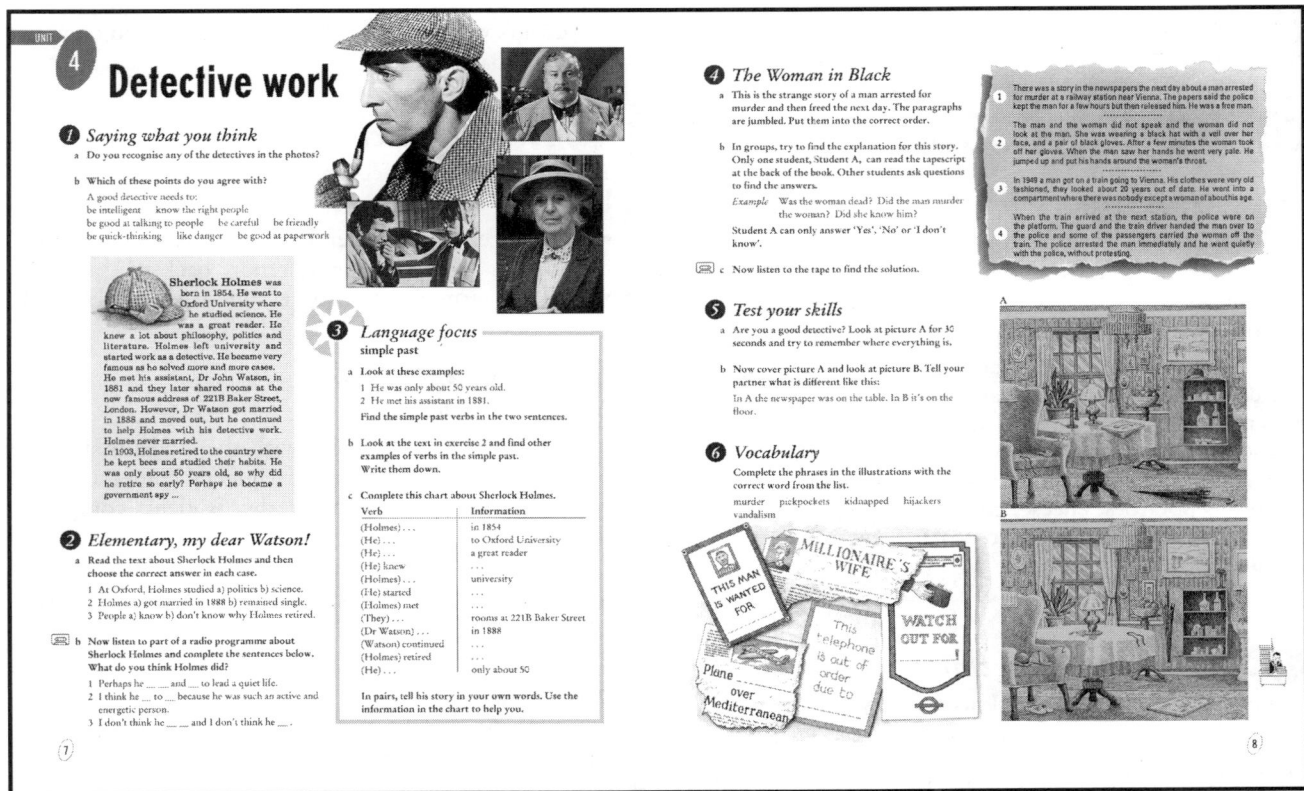

S ⑤ Test your skills ⊖

Remembering the contents of a picture and then telling partners about the differences between two pictures.

a • Pre-teach new vocabulary.
  • Students study the picture for 30 seconds.
b • In pairs, students work to compile and note down a list of differences.
⊕ • Pairs of students team up with another pair and check/extend their list.

Answer key

Picture A	Picture B
shoes in the cupboard	shoes under the chair
newspaper on the table	newspaper on the floor
tie on the chair	tie on the table
watch on the newspaper	watch on the arm of the chair
umbrella on the floor	umbrella hanging on the cupboard doorknob
hats on the top of the cupboard	hats on seat of the chair
bottles on the middle shelf of the cupboard	bottles on the top shelf of the cupboard
pipe on the chair	pipe on the table
phone on the table	phone on the top of the cupboard
pair of glasses on the arm of the chair	glasses on the newspaper on the floor

R·W ⑥ Vocabulary ⊖

Matching exercise.
• Students complete the phrases. Allow them to use their dictionaries.
⊕ • Students suggest other types of crime/criminals, eg. mugger.

Answer key
murder kidnapped pickpockets vandalism hijacked

Extension activities

1 Reading
Students read a graded reader of their choice.

2 Writing
Students write a paragraph about their own life history. Students' writing will need to be guided.

TEACHER'S NOTES

Unit 5
Eating for health

Aims
Structures: adverbs of frequency and their position
Functions: offering, accepting and refusing food
Lexis: chocolate, spots, bananas, energy, carrots, rice, fat, healthy, vegetarian, teenage, overweight, cereal, sugar, left-over, fried, chicken, chips, packet, biscuits, take-away, fresh, vegetables, exercise, regularly, embarrassed, depressed, butter, potatoes, cheese, pasta, raw, yoghurt, steak, professional, dancer, toast, night club, juice, lemon

S ❶ *Saying what you think*
Discussing the effects of various foods.
a • Make sure students understand the vocabulary.
b • One student from each pair tells the class what he/she thought and why.
⊕ • Students make a list of the foods they like or don't like. Then they note which of the foods on their list are good for them. They discuss their findings with a partner.

R·W ❷ *Health break*
Reading about a teenager's eating habits.
a • Make sure students understand that a health farm is somewhere that people go to diet/exercise/get healthy.
• Before students read the text, put some of their suggestions for words on the board.
b • If necessary use a couple of examples to explain 'good habit' (eg exercising) and 'bad habit' (eg eating a lot of chocolate).
• Students read the text again and make their lists. Write lists on the board. Students extend the list with their own bad habits - you can limit their suggestions to diet and health, or extend them to include other types of bad habit, eg nail biting.
Answer key
Karen's bad habits: She used to eat too much, she ate the wrong foods, she never ate fruit and she rarely had fresh vegetables. She didn't exercise.
c • Students match paragraphs with topic headings.
Answer key
a 3, b 1, c 4, d 5

⊕ • Students write a list of their good habits and compare it with a partner's.

S ❸ *Health Check*
Asking questions to complete a questionnaire about health and fitness.
a • Students can move round the class asking questions or work in groups. Students report back to the class.
⊕ • Students write 2 more survey questions of their own.

❹ *Language focus*
Adverbs of frequency.
a • Go through the examples with the students. Elicit/point out that the adverb of frequency comes after the verb *to be* but before other verbs. Students complete the rule.
b • Students complete the chart. Of course, the percentages are only approximate guides to when the adverbs should be used.
• Students find the adverbs in exercise 2.
Answer key
0 - never, 10 - rarely, 35 - sometimes, 65 - often, 80 - usually, 100 - always
⊕ Give students examples of things you often/rarely etc do. Use prompts on the board to elicit similar examples from the students.
c • Students put the adverb in the correct place in the sentences.
Answer key
1 Overweight teenagers *usually* eat the wrong kind of food.
2 They are *often* depressed about their weight.
3 They *rarely* eat fresh fruit and vegetables.
4 Karen *never* ate fruit when she was younger.
5 She *always* bought chocolate at break time.
6 Do you *sometimes* eat the wrong kind of food?
⊕ • Students use each adverb to write a sentence about their good and bad habits.

S·L ❺ *A dancer's diet* ⊖
Listening to a dancer talk about her diet and answering questions.
a • Elicit/point out that a dancer needs to stay slim and healthy and needs energy.
• Students note down the foods they think a dancer eats. Let them use their dictionaries. Put their suggestions on the board.
b • Students listen to the tape and note down the foods Gill says she eats. Compare what's on the tape with the suggestions on the board.

TEACHER'S NOTES

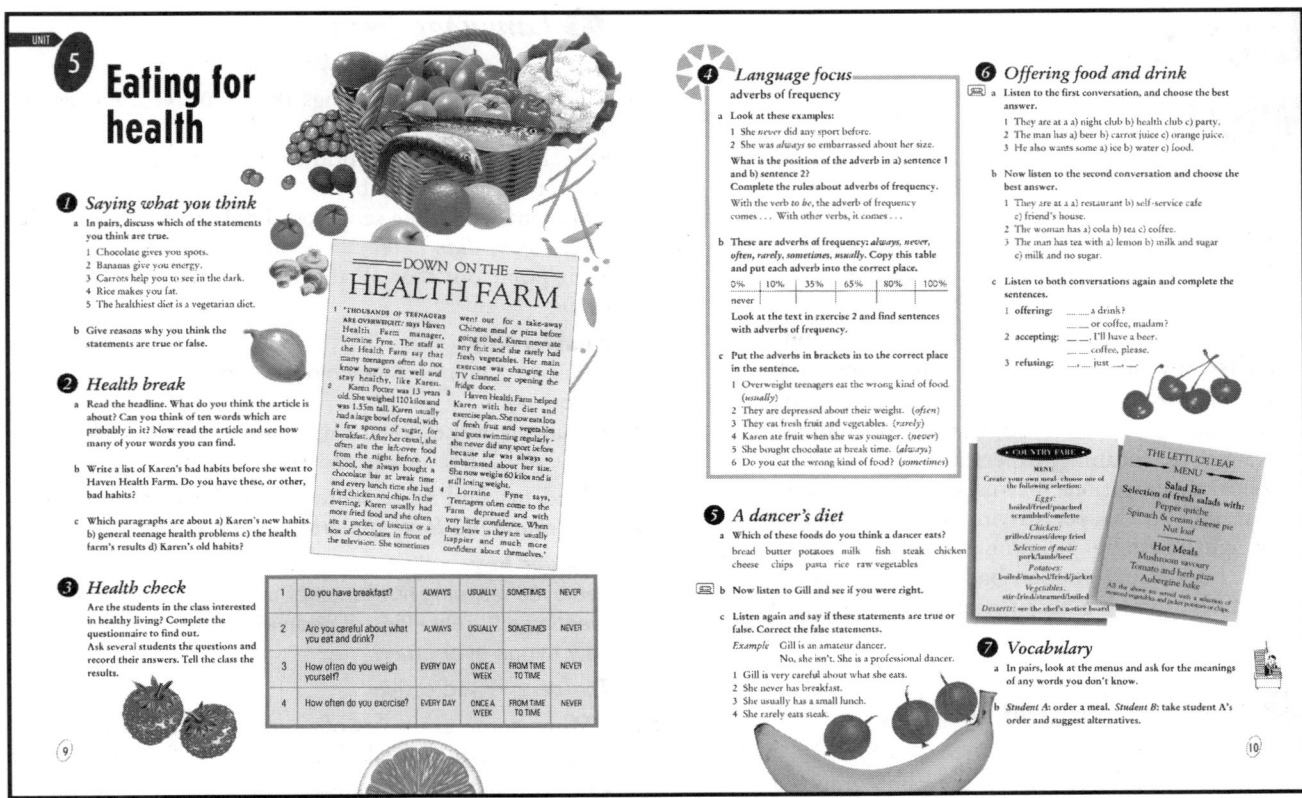

Answer key
Gill eats all these foods, but not much red meat.

c Play the tape again for students to answer the true/false questions.

⊕ • Students suggest 3 other people and then say what type of food they eat, eg. *boxer - red meat, eggs, pasta; model - fresh vegetables, fruit*.

Answer key
1 F (She eats what she wants.)   2 F (She always has breakfast.)   3 F (She never has lunch.)   4 T, 5 T, 6 F (She used to weigh 40 kilos.)

L ⑥ *Offering food and drink*
Listening to two short conversations on offering and accepting/refusing food and drink.

a,b • Students listen to the conversations and answer the multiple choice questions.

Answer key
a 1 b   2 c   3 a
b 1 a   2 c   3 a

c • Students listen again and complete the sentences.
⊕ • Write some more sentences on the board and ask students to complete them.

Answer key
1 a How about ...?   b Would you like ....?
2 a Yes, please...   b I'll have...
3 a No, not...now thanks.

S ⑦ *Vocabulary* ⊖
Vocabulary extension. Discussing menus.

a • Students in groups check the meanings of the words they don't know.
⊕ • Students choose the menu they prefer and say why.
⊕ • Students suggest a type of eating place, eg cafe, fast food takeaway, pub, health food restaurant, and then write a menu for it.

b • Provide the first 2 sentences of the dialogue for the students. Remind them of key phrases and give them plenty of time to practise.

Extension activities
1 Planning a menu
Students plan a menu. Each student must have one dish from their country on the menu.
2 True or false
In pairs, students make statements like those in exercise 1 a. The other students guess if they are true or false.

TEACHER'S NOTES

Unit 6
What a job!

Aims
Structures: *love, like, enjoy, didn't like* + gerund; *too/very* + adjective
Functions: describing activities you like and dislike, asking for meaning, talking about jobs
Lexis: army, keen on, career, outdoors, hard, training, recruits, abroad, flexible, open-minded, dangerous, meaning, experience(d), cook, tour guide, qualifications, exams, diplomas, circus, assistant, zoo-keeper, driving licence, model, earn, (weight) training, swimming, waiting, day(s) off, age, busker, entertainer, bad weather, spring, summer, thinking about, experience, salary, staff

S ### 1 *Saying what you think*
Discussing jobs.

a • Students discuss the jobs in the photographs and decide what they are. Encourage them to use the phrases in the examples.
⊕ • Students list as many jobs as they can think of in 2 minutes. Make a class list.
Answer key
busker, dancer, model

R·W ### 2 *Army life*
Reading a text about a woman captain in the army and answering questions.

a • Students read the text through once quickly and tell you where it is from, giving reasons for their answers.
Answer key
b An army information booklet. It's purpose is to persuade readers that the army would be a good career.

b • Write students' answers to question 1 on the board.
• Students discuss the answers to 2 and 3 and then tell the class what they have decided.
Answer key
1 **She likes**: teaching and helping recruits, travelling and learning how other armies work.

c • Students make their lists. Write a class list on the board.
⊕ • Choose one of the jobs from exercise 1. Students tell you what the good and bad points of the job are.

3 *Language focus*
Love, like, enjoy, didn't like + gerund.

⊕ a • Tell students about things that you *like, love, enjoy, didn't like* doing.
• Focus students' attention on the gerunds in the answer to question 2 b 1.
• Students complete sentences 1-5. Put the phrases *like, love, enjoy, didn't like* + gerund on the board and elicit/point out that all the words after the verb end in *-ing*.
Answer key
1 being   2 being   3 teaching, helping   4 travelling
5 working
⊕ • Students write down three things they *like, love, enjoy, don't like* doing and then tell the class.

b • Students find more sentences in the text with verbs *like, enjoy* and *love*, underlining the gerund.
Answer key
I enjoyed *learning* how another army worked. Do you like *meeting* different kinds of people? Do you enjoy *learning* new things every day?

Too/very + adjective.

⊕ a • Mime some examples of your own: eg I'm too hot/cold/tired/sad/worried. I'm very happy/hungry.
a,b • Go through the examples with students, explaining the difference between too and very - *too* is used when there is more of a particular quality than wanted or desired, e.g. *too* dangerous, *too* helpful.
Answer key
1 too   2 very   3 very   4 very, too

L·S ### 4 *Position vacant*
Practising asking for and explaining the meaning of words.

a • Before listening, read through the advertisements with the students. Go over the essential vocabulary only.
Answer key
1, for a cook, 4, for a tour guide.

b • Students listen to the questions and explanations again and fill in the gaps.
Answer key
1 What does ...mean?   2 It means ...   3 Can you ... the meaning?   4 Its ... same as ...

c • Students note the words they don't know and take turns asking the class or teacher their meaning. Focus on correct use of functional language for asking for and explaining meaning.
⊕ • Discuss other ways students deal with difficult vocabulary: use a dictionary, ignore it, etc.

TEACHER'S NOTES

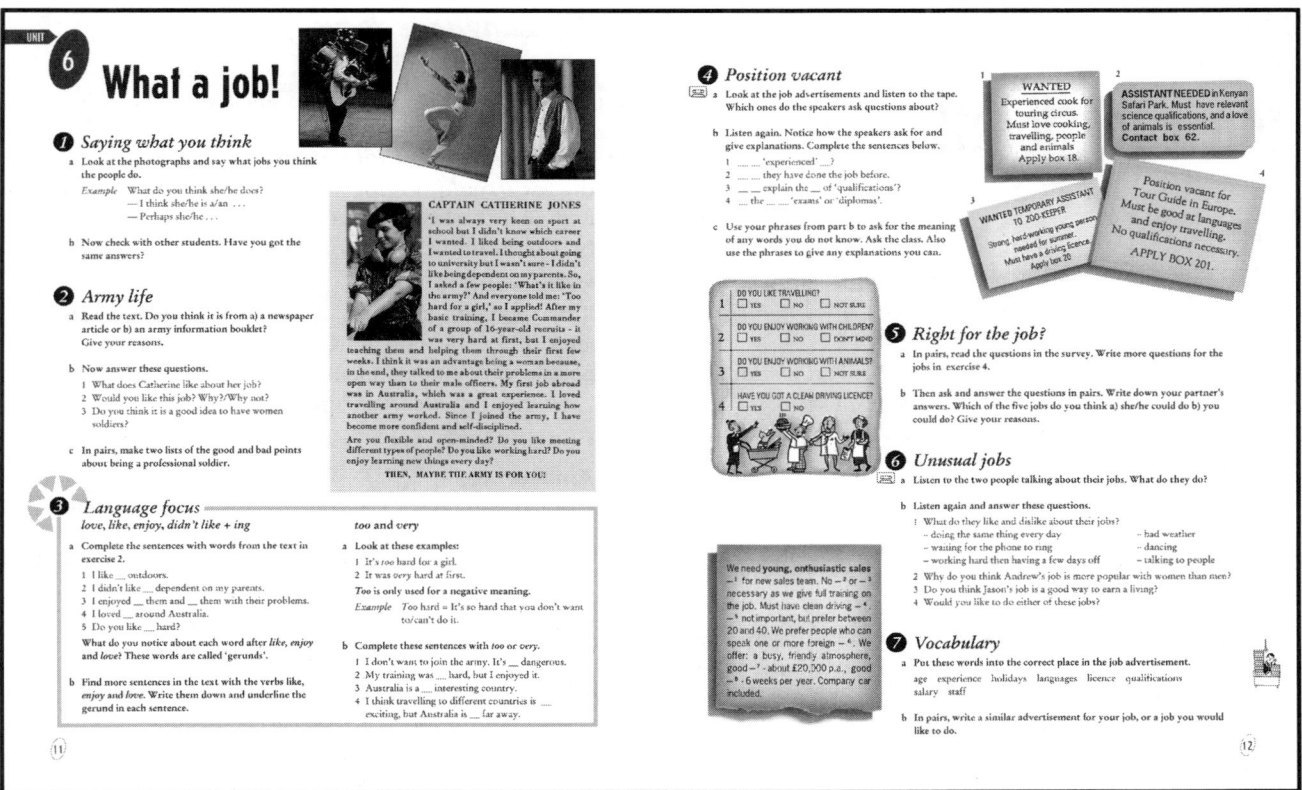

W·S ⑤ Right for the job?
Writing and asking questions in pairs for a survey

a • Go through the questions with students. Make sure they understand the difference between 'not sure' (don't know) and 'don't mind' (no strong feelings).
• In pairs, students write their questions.

b • Students change partners to conduct their survey.
• A few students tell the class which job their partner or they could do and why.

⊕ • Students suggest other jobs they or their partner could do and give reasons for their choices.

L·W ⑥ Unusual jobs
Listening to two speakers describe unusual jobs and answering questions about what they say.

a • Play the tape, pausing between speakers for students to identify what they do.

b • Play the tape, in short sections if necessary, for students to listen and take notes.
• Students answer questions as a group. Write up their suggestions on the board.

Answer key
a Speaker 1, Andrew, is a male model. Speaker 2, Jason, is a busker, or street entertainer.
b **Andrew likes**: working hard and then having a few days off. **doesn't like**: waiting for the phone to ring.

Jason likes: dancing, talking to people; **doesn't like**: bad weather.

W ⑦ Vocabulary
Understanding vocabulary used in job advertisements. Writing a job advertisement.

a • Students read through the job advertisement first. Go over new vocabulary before students complete the text.

Answer key
staff, experience, qualifications, licence, age, languages, salary, holidays

⊕ b • Choose a job and write an advertisement on the board with the class.
• Students decide what job they would like to do and tell the class.
• Students can write the actual advertisement in class or for homework.

Extension activities

1 Vocabulary extension work
Different jobs: the job and the person who does it eg teaching/teacher.

2 Job crossword
Students are given a completed job crossword and they write the clues for it.

TEACHER'S NOTES

Unit 7
You can do it!

Aims
Structures: *can* and *couldn't* for ability
Functions: talking about languages; making and disagreeing with suggestions
Lexis: communicating, universal language, a short time, symbols, signs, anyone, system, experts, computer, translation, character, simple, alphabet, letter, sound, understand, code

S ❶ *Saying what you think*
Discussing ways of communicating.

a • Students identify the ways of communicating in the illustration. Students tell you which, if any, of the ways of communicating they can read or understand.
⊕ • Elicit other ways of communicating: speech, pictures, noises, etc.

Answer key
shorthand   music   backward writing   colour blindness test card   sign language   computer language

b • Students tell you what other students can do.

R·W ❷ *Universal language*
Reading a text about a universal language and answering comprehension questions.

⊕ • Find out what languages students in the class speak. Write up a list on the board. Explain that 'universal language' is a language that everyone speaks.

a • Students read the text once through quickly.

Answer key
He has created a universal language to help people, like himself, who have had to learn a language in a very short time.

b • Students read the text in more detail and answer question 1.
• In pairs, students discuss the answers to 2 and 3 and report back to the class.

Answer key
1 *50:* Mr Zavalani emigrated from Albania fifty years ago.
30: the number of years he spent writing the language.
600: the number of symbols in his language.
30: the number of hours it takes to learn his language.
300: the number of years people have spent trying to write a universal language.
a million: the number of people who speak Esperanto.

❸ *Language focus*
can/could for ability

a • Look at the examples and elicit that *can* refers to present ability, while *could* refers to past ability.
⊕ • Build up a substitution table on the board to clarify that *can/could* do not need the auxiliaries *do/does/did*, and also to show students that *can* is always followed by the infinitive form of the verb, without *to*.

b • **Answer key**
'I *couldn't* find a job ...' ... *could* he perhaps use this idea ...? 'Anyone *can* learn my language ...' ... to people who *cannot* speak ... 'Why *can't* teachers teach ... so that American children *can* ...?

c • Students can work individually or in pairs.

Answer key
1 Could you speak English when you were a child?
2 How many languages can you speak?
3 Mr Zavalani could not find a job because he could not speak English.
4 How many people can speak Esperanto?
5 We can not translate everything by computers.

⊕ d • Introduce by miming/demonstrating what you can and can't do now. (e.g. *I can drive but I can't draw.*) and what you could/couldn't do when you were a child (e.g. *I could run, but I couldn't swim.*)
• Look at the example with the students. Get them to tell you what they can/can't do now and could/couldn't do when they were children. Elicit 'I can ...now, but I couldn't ... when I was a child.'
• Students find out what their partner can/can't do now and could/couldn't do and make lists. They then tell the class about their partner.

R·S·W ❹ *Writing in pictographs* ⊖
Translating symbols or pictographs and creating symbols.

a • Pairs work out the meaning of the symbols and report back to the class.

b • Pairs write their own pictograph symbols and show them to another pair to try to guess what they mean.

L·W ❺ *Can you read Japanese?* ⊖
Listening to someone describe what it is like to learn Japanese and answering comprehension questions.

a • Ask students if they think Japanese is an easy or a difficult language to learn. Make sure they understand the difference between characters, which represent a word or idea, and an alphabet, where letters represent sounds. Students listen to the tape and answer questions 1 and 2.

TEACHER'S NOTES

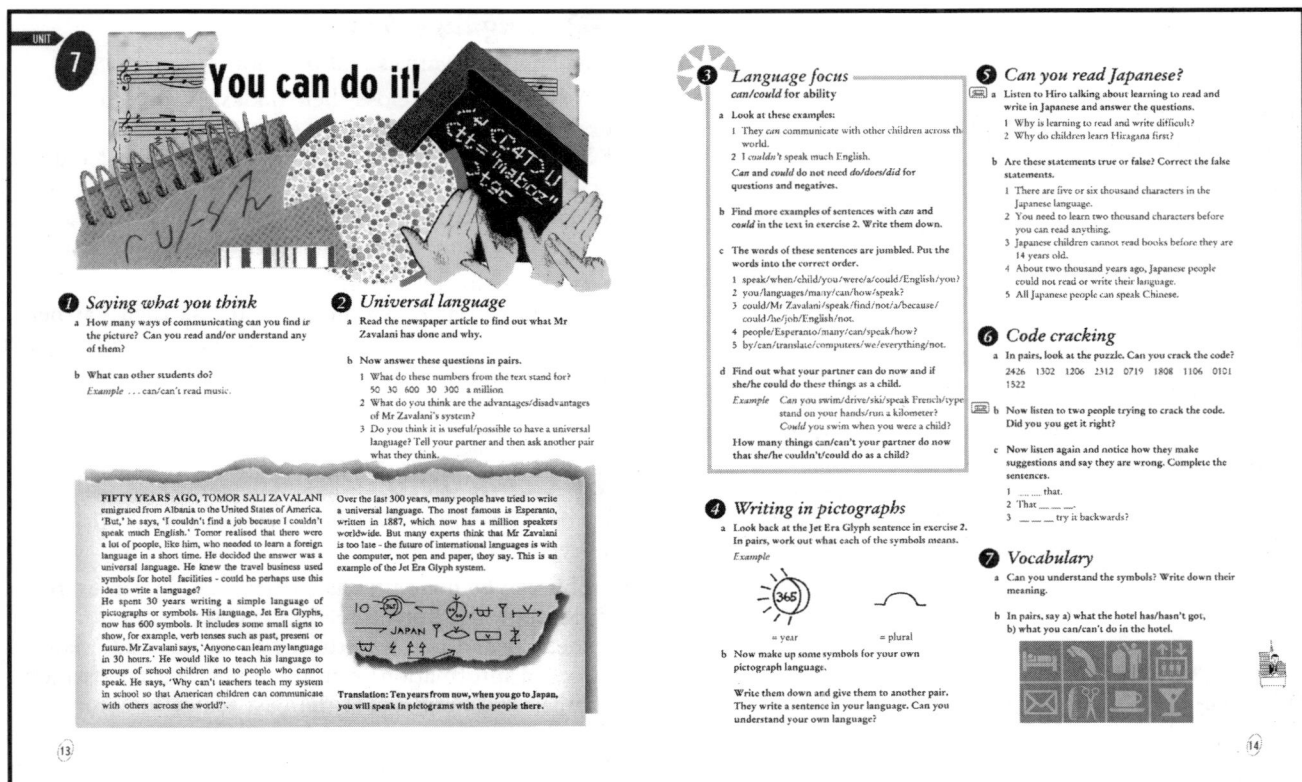

Answer key
1 It's difficult because there are so many characters and symbols to learn. 2 They learn Hiragana first because it's a simple alphabet. So, children can learn to read quickly.

b • Students can try to answer the T/F questions from memory.
• Play the tape again in sections for students to check their answers in pairs.

Answer key
1 T 2 F (You need to learn 800 characters.) 3 F (They use a simpler alphabet for reading before they are 14.) 4 T 5 F (They can read Chinese, but they can't speak it.)

L·S·W ❻ Code cracking
Trying to 'crack' a code. Focussing on the language of making and rejecting suggestions.

a • Pairs try to understand the code. Students report back to the class.

b • Students listen to the tape. If they still don't understand the code, demonstrate for them on the board.

Answer key
Decoded, the numbers read: Can you do this puzzle?

c • Play the tape again for students to complete the sentences.

⊕ • Give students some other puzzles to work on, in groups, to practise the language of suggestion.

Answer key
1 let's try... 2 can't be right.. 3 Why don't we...

R·S ❼ Vocabulary ⊖
Understanding symbols for hotel facilities.

a • Students write down English equivalents for the symbols.

Answer key
lift laundry telephone bedroom bar coffee shop hairdressers post

b • Ask pairs to tell the class what the hotel has/hasn't got and what you can/can't do there.

⊕ • Students decode other common signs/symbols, eg *No Smoking, No Parking, Restaurant,* etc.

Extension activities
1 Survey
Students compile a list of activities and find out how many other people in the class can do the activities on their list.
2 Code cracking
Groups write codes and others try to 'crack' them.

TEACHER'S NOTES

Unit 8
Twenties' fever

Aims
Structures: negative and question forms of the past simple tense
Functions: asking questions and giving information about past events
Lexis: style, twenties, magic tricks, emigrated, trapeze artist, immediately, tied, chains, locked, prison cell, escaped, threw, tramp, walking stick, communist, events, entertainment, economics, fashion, transport, history, disaster, tomb, gold, jewels, mask, cartoon, financial market, collapsed, alive, remember, fridge, washing machine, modern, millions, decade, century

S **1** *Saying what you think*
Discussing famous people in the 1920's. Comparing styles then and now.

a • Elicit what the students know about the people in the photographs. If they don't recognise the people, see what they can guess about them from the information in the photograph. (The people are: Charlie Chaplin, Suzanne Lenglen, Lenin, Amy Jonson)

b • Elicit differences in fashion, entertainment, lifestyle, for example.

S **2** *The greatest escapologist*
Reading and answering questions about Harry Houdini.

a • Ask students what they know about Harry Houdini. Students discuss the photo. Put their answers and suggestions about his life on the board.
• Students read the text through quickly, only to find the answer to the gist question, ie what he was famous for.

Answer key
He was famous for his escaping tricks.

b • Students read the text more carefully and answer the questions.

⊕ • In pairs, students retell the story of Harry Houdini. One or two students retell it for the class.

Answer key
1 Ehrich Weiss.   2 He worked as a trapeze artist, as a magician and as an escapologist.   3 He escaped from prison cells and from a wooden box tied with chains.

3 *Language focus*
Past simple negatives and questions

a • Ask students to close their books. Write the 2 examples on the board.
• Students suggest why *did* is used in example 2 and not in example 1.
• Make sure that they realise that the main verb is not in the past tense form when the auxiliary *did* is used.

b • Students do this exercise in pairs.

⊕ • Students prepare 3-5 questions to ask their partner about his past. Students interview one another in pairs.

Answer key
1a 2f 3a 4g 5c 6b 7e

R·W **4** *Comic hero*
Using notes about Charlie Chaplin to write his life story.

⊕ • This can be done first as an information gap exercise. Photocopy the notes, creating two sets - one for student A and one for student B. Remove alternate pieces of information from the notes. Students ask one another questions (using the past tense) to complete their sets of notes.
• Students individually or in pairs write about Charlie Chaplin from the notes. Encourage them to use the text about Harry Houdini as a model.
• For weaker classes, ask pairs of students to write sentences using information from one or two of the notes only. Then all the students' contributions are put together to produce a text.

⊕ • Write 3 facts about a famous historical figure on the board (make sure all the class are likely to know this person) but don't give his/her name. In pairs, students prepare three questions in the past to ask and guess who the person is.

L **5** *The roaring twenties* ⊖
Listening to a man talk about his life in the 1920's and answering questions.

a • Students listen once and identify the fact that he mentions the Wall Street Crash.

b • Students try to answer the true or false questions from memory, before listening again. Students compare their answers in pairs.

Answer key
1T 2F 3T 4F 5T 6F 7T

⊕ • Students write 2 sentences each about events in the past. The class guess if they are true or false and correct them. Write an example on the board first, e.g. *The first man landed on the moon in 1956. World War II started in 1914.*

15

Teacher's Notes

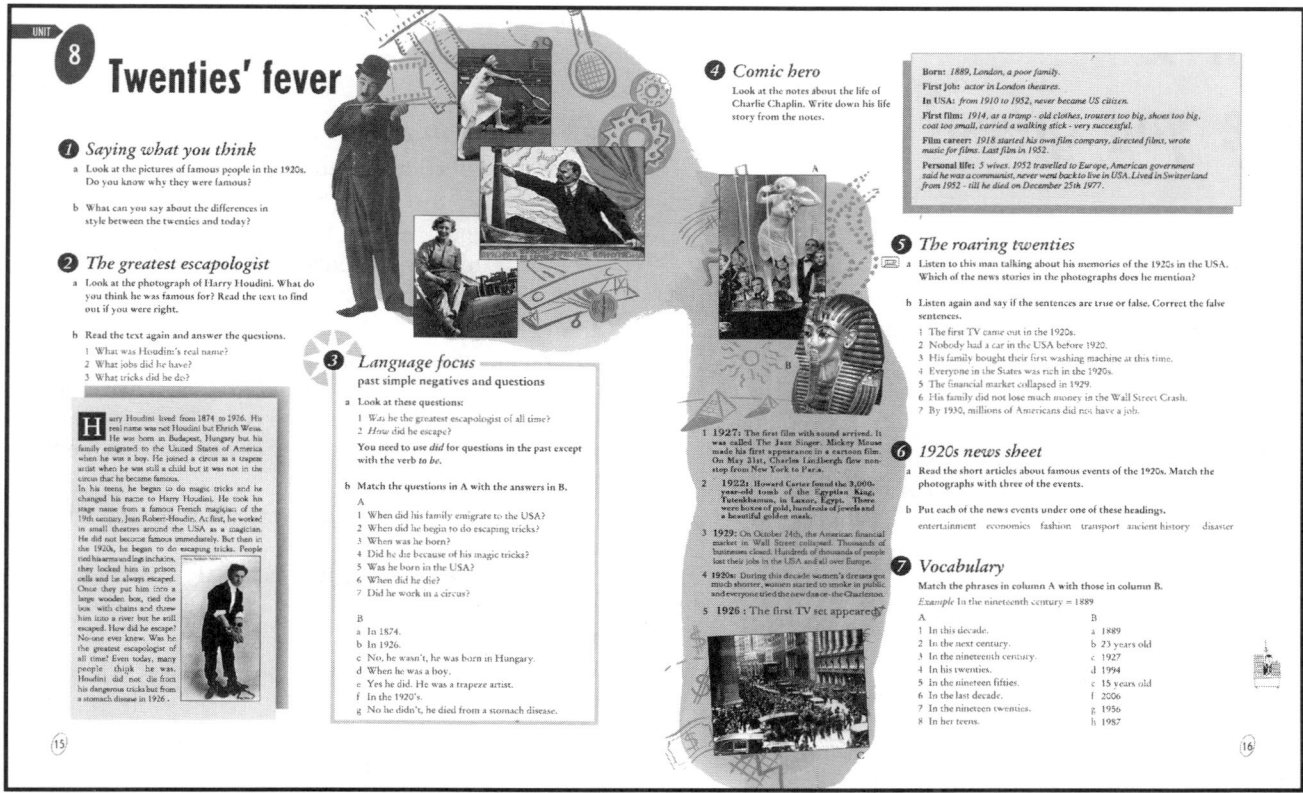

R ⑥ 1920s news sheet

Matching short news articles to headings.

a • Students look at the photographs and tell you what they see/what they think is happening in each.
• Students read through the news events and match them with the photographs.

Answer key
Text 2 - photo A   Text 3 - photo C   Text 4 - Photo B

b • Make sure students understand the headings. Let them use their dictionaries if necessary.
• Students match the events with the headings.
✚ • Put some recent events under the headings and/or clip out some more recent stories from newspapers. Students place those under the same headings.

Answer key
entertainment: 1926 - first TV set, 1927 - first film with sound; **economics:** 1929 - Wall Street Crash; **fashion:** 1920's - women's dresses got shorter; **transport:** 1927 - Charles Lindbergh's flight from NY to Paris; **ancient history:** 1922 - discovery of Tutankhamen's tomb; **disaster:** - 1929 Wall Street Crash

R·W ⑦ Vocabulary

Matching dates with descriptions of periods of time.
• Make sure students understand *decade* and *century*.
• Students match the phrases with dates.

✚ • Go through the phrases and dates with students, concentrating on the word stress in the phrases in A and how to read the dates in B.

Answer key
1 d   2 f   3 a   4 b   5 g   6 h   7 c   8 e

Extension activities

1 Profile
Students write a short paragraph about a famous person they know of, preferably one from their own country. If the person is still alive encourage students to write about his/her past.

2 News sheet
Students choose a decade and write sentences for each of the headings in 6b.

TEACHER'S NOTES

Unit 9
Are you green?

Aims
Structures: the imperative in affirmative and negative forms
Functions: giving and following directions, asking for and giving opinions, agreeing and disagreeing
Lexis: litter, traffic, factory, waste, noise, environment, leaflet, plastic, container, public transport, unleaded petrol, switch off, electric, writing, put on, look for, recycled, rubbish, directions, beetle, sport, organise, gas fuel, engine, power, disposable, spray

S **1** *Saying what you think*
Discussing types of pollution.

a • Students identify the types of pollution in the illustration and say which one they think is the most dangerous and why.

b • Students discuss their concerns about the environment.

R **2** *What can you do?*
Reading a leaflet about ways to help the environment and choosing the correct verb form.

a • Go through the text with students explaining new vocabulary.
• Students work together selecting the correct verb form.
• Discuss the correct answers

Answer key
Don't buy   Teach   travel   Don't take ... use   don't get   Switch off   put on   Don't wear   look for   Don't throw   take   use

b • Discuss which rules students follow and why or why not.
• In pairs, students think of at least one more rule and read their suggestions aloud to the class. Class vote on the best suggestion(s).
• Students suggest which rules they agree or disagree with.

Answer key
Possible rules
Take empty bottles to bottle banks.
Separate rubbish to make recycling easier.
Cycle to work.

Don't use aerosol sprays.
Don't put too much water in the bath.

L·S **3** *Green maze*
Following directions given by two speakers. Giving directions.

a • Give students a minute to study the maze and ask any questions. In pairs students find the way out of the maze to the green field.

Answer key
Go straight ahead and take the second turning on the left. Turn right after the statue, and go straight ahead. Turn left and take the first turning on the right. Then take the first turning on the left, walk straight ahead and you meet the green fields.

b • Explain that a rubbish collector is someone who takes away your rubbish.
• Play the tape, pausing it if necessary for students to follow the directions.

Answer key
Speaker A leads you to the rubbish. Speaker B leads you to the glass.

c • Play the tape again for students to identify which speakers use which phrases.

Answer key
Speaker A - phrases 1 and 4. Speaker B - phrases 2 and 3.

d • Students take turns giving directions in pairs.
⊕ • To check the activity, have one or two students give their directions to the class and see if the others can follow them.

4 *Language focus*
The imperative.

a • Look at the examples with the students, identifying the verbs and discussing which is positive and which is negative.
• Ask students to give you other examples of suggestions or advice in the imperative form.
⊕ • Elicit possible uses of the imperative form, ie in advice, directions, instructions, rules, etc.
⊕ • Students go back to the text in exercise 2 and write down all the imperative verbs in 2 columns under the headings *positive* and *negative*.

b • Complete the first line as a class to ensure students understand the task.
• Students work together completing the text.

Answer key
1 don't take   2 go   3 Don't spend   4 save   5 Don't waste   6 be   7 wear   8 don't forget

Teacher's Notes

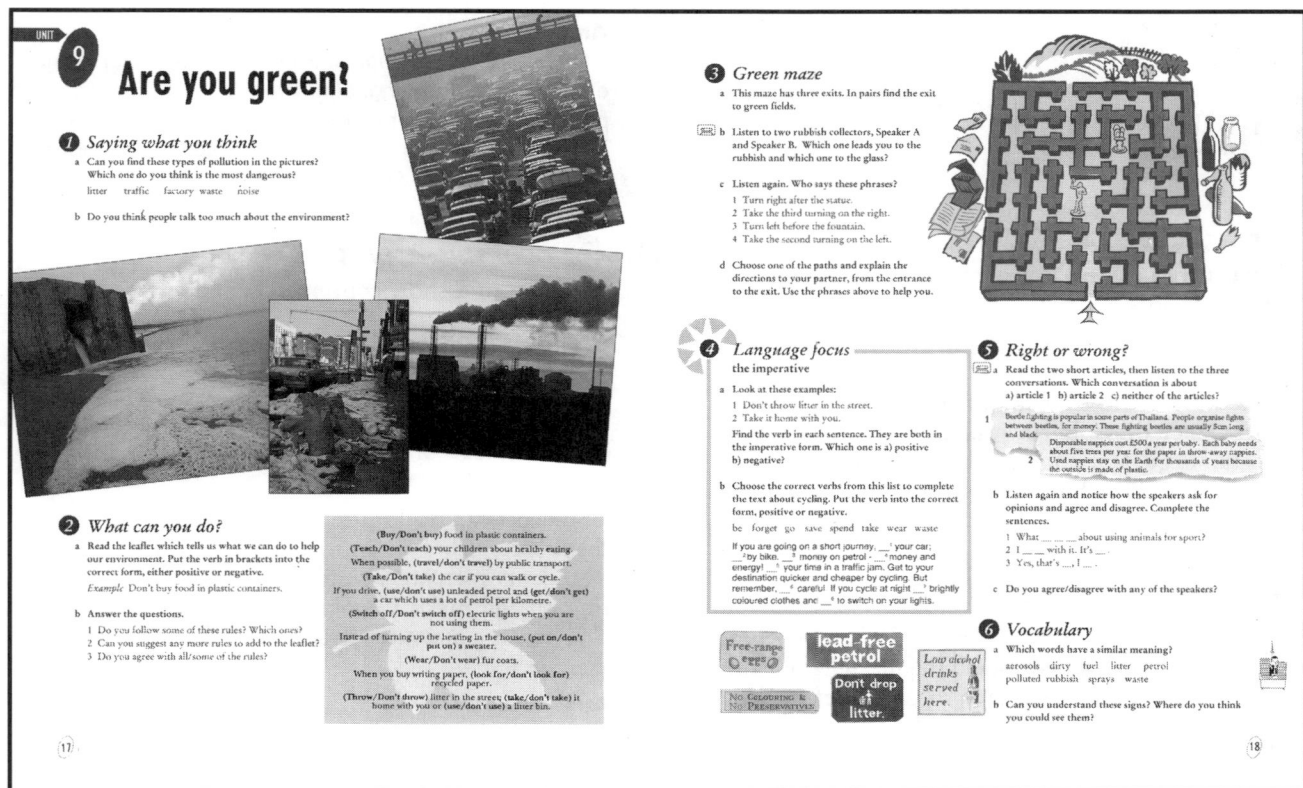

L·W·S ⑤ *Right or wrong?*

Matching conversations to related texts. Focussing on language for asking for and giving ideas and opinions and language for agreeing and disagreeing.

a • Students read the short articles. Make sure they understand the vocabulary, particularly 'beetle' and 'nappy'.
• Students listen to the conversations and match them with the texts.

Answer key
article 1 - dialogue A; article 2 - dialogue C

b • Students listen again and complete the sentences.

Answer key
1 ... do you think?   2 ... don't agree ... wrong   3 ... right ... agree

c • Using the information on the tape, put prompts on board for students to ask and state opinions about and for other students to agree or disagree with. Make a note of the phrases on the board.
⊕ • Students use the prompts and phrases on the board to prepare and practise short dialogues.

R·W ⑥ *Vocabulary* ⊖

Revising vocabulary relating to pollution. Understanding signs.

a • Students match the words with a similar meaning.

Answer key
a aerosols - sprays; dirty - polluted; fuel - petrol; litter - rubbish

b • Students explain the signs and say where they might be found.

Answer key
in the street, at a petrol station, on a food packet, in a supermarket, in a pub, club.

Extension activities

1 Do's and dont's
Students use the vocabulary in Unit 5 to write a list of do's and don'ts for healthy eating.

2 Poster
Students prepare a poster on the theme of protecting the environment.

3 Spidergram
Students do a spidergram around the word *pollution*.

TEACHER'S NOTES

Unit 10
Leisure time

Aims
Structures: the present continuous for future arrangements
Functions: making, accepting and refusing invitations
Lexis: leisure, free time, murder, hobby, standard, hire, fancy dress, killer, jealous, regret, balcony, costume, guide, pottery, sightseeing, parachuting, tour, ancient, architecture

S **1** *Saying what you think*
Discussing leisure and leisure activities.

a • Make sure students understand the meaning of *leisure time* and *hobby*. Students name the activities in the pictures. Put their suggestions on the board.
• Students ask and tell their partners what they do in their free time: fishing, having a meal/eating out, reading, going to the cinema, dancing, playing football.

b • In a multinational class students can be grouped according to nationality. Students mark the statements true or false. Discuss the results as a class.

⊕ • Students write one or two sentences each about the way they/people in general spend their leisure time in their country and read their sentence(s) aloud to the class.

R·W **2** *Murder is my hobby*
Reading about a murder weekend and answering questions.

a • Tell the class that '... is my hobby.' and write the sentence on the board as a model. Ask one or two students to finish the sentence for themselves.

⊕ • Focus on the title of the section. Introduce the concept of murder, i.e. to take the life of another human being. Discuss ways of murdering someone, eg poisoning, stabbing them.

a • Students read the text quickly and answer the questions.

Answer key
a 1 b) an advertisement   2 Guests can help to solve a murder mystery.

b • Students compare their answers with a partner, followed by class discussion.

⊕ • Students say if they would like to go on a Murder Weekend and give reasons for their answers.

Answer key
1 Quality Hotel   2 Begins: Friday evening, after dinner; ends: Sunday morning, after breakfast.   3 The standard price includes a room (without a balcony), a private bath or shower, a colour TV, phone and radio.   4 Children under 16.   5 £34   6 Telephone the hotel.

L·W **3** *Booking a place*
Listening to a short conversation and answering questions.

a • Students read the questions and listen to the conversation.

Answer key
On Friday 13th   2 A double room without a balcony
3 £155 + £34 + £6 = £195

b • Students can read through the phrases and try to join them before they listen to the tape again.

⊕ • Students roleplay a similar conversation where they ring up and make a booking for a Murder Weekend. You can use a similar structure to that of Unit 3, exercise 6.

Answer key
1b 2e 3g 4d 5f 6a 7c

4 *Language focus*
The present continuous for future arrangements.

⊕ • Talk about your own plans/arrangements for the weekend. Eg *I'm visiting some friends this weekend. They live in .... I'm driving up on Friday evening.*

⊕ • Ask other students what they're doing at the weekend. Build up a substitution table on the board.

a • Look at the two examples. Establish that the sentences are referring to the future.

b • Ask and answer one or two questions about Mrs Valentine's arrangements with the students.
• Students work in pairs asking and answering questions.

⊕ • Students close their books and one or two students tell the class about Mrs Valentine's arrangements.

⊕ • In pairs, students ask one another about their plans/arrangements for the evening or weekend and then tell the class.

Answer key
All the sentences in 3b are examples of the present continuous used to describe fixed plans and arrangements.

R·S·L **5** *Going out*
Reading advertisements and listening to short conversations. Focussing on language for inviting, accepting and refusing.

a • Go through the advertisements with the students. Elicit what events are being advertised.

19

TEACHER'S NOTES

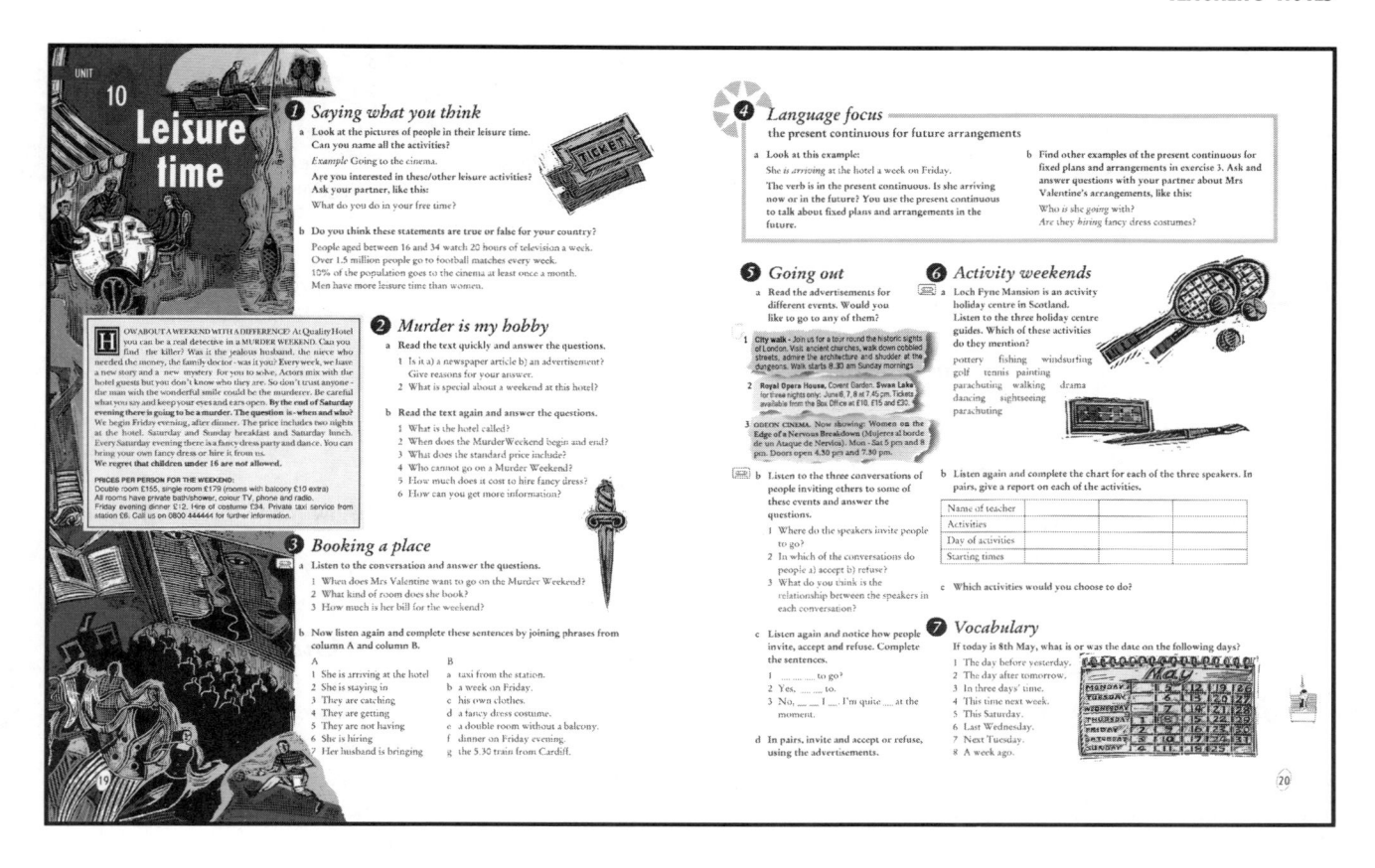

b • Play the conversations, pausing between each for the students to answer the questions.

Answer key
1 A: a walk around the city   B: the ballet   C: a Spanish film   2 They accept in A & C and refuse in B.

c • Students listen again to complete the sentences.

Answer key
1 Would you like...?   2 ...I'd love to   3 ...I'm afraid I can't. ...busy...

d • Make sure students understand that when they refuse an invitation it is polite to give a reason.
• Build up a short conversation on the board, modeled on one of the dialogues.
• Students roleplay in pairs, and then one or two pairs act out their roleplays for the class.

L·W·S ❻ Activity weekends

Listening for information on activity holidays and completing a chart.

a • Explain 'activity holiday centre', ie a place you go to have a holiday and do hobbies/activities. Ensure students understand the vocabulary.
• Students listen to the guides and note the activities.

Answer key
walking, sightseeing, pottery, golf, parachuting.

b • Students complete the chart for each of the speakers. Encourage them to use the present continuous tense when they report each of the activities.

Answer key

Name of teacher:	Maggie	Ian	Chris
Activities:	walking, sightseeing	pottery	golf
Day of activities:	Saturday	Saturday	Sunday
Starting times:	10.00	9.30	10.30

c • Students say which activities they would like to do.

❼ Vocabulary

Vocabulary for dates.

• This can be done either as a class activity or competitively ie the student that finishes first 'wins'.

Answer key
1 6th May 2 10th May 3 11th May 4 15th May
6 1st May

Extension activities

1 Word web
Students start a word web with hobby at the centre.

2 Hobbies
Students write 2 or 3 sentences about their favourite hobby/activity and why they enjoy it.

TEACHER'S NOTES

Unit 11
My own business

Aims
Structures: *How much? How many?*, tense revision
Functions: sympathising and congratulating
Lexis: business, idea, education, success, luck, partner, confidence, work out, decisions, team, competition, cheque, prize, advice/adviser, ties, exam (revision) papers, orders, profit, charge, project, glass, company, previous, invested, funding, main, customer, graduate, travel agency, persuaded, loan, run (a business), venture, make a loss

S **1** *Saying what you think*
Discussing what is required to start your own business.
a • Make sure students understand the notion of starting your own business. Without looking at the list, students suggest what they think is required and why. Write their suggestions on the board.
b • Discuss the vocabulary with the students, before they work in pairs.
 • One or two students report their decisions back to the class and say why they made those choices.

L·S·W **2** *Youth enterprise*
Listening to information about a Youth Enterprise scheme and to conversations about starting up your own business.
a • Encourage students to work out the answer to the question by looking at the words *youth* and *enterprise*. Allow them to use their dictionaries. Put their suggestions on the board before you play the tape.
 • Play Part 1 of the tape. Put relevant words or phrases that students can remember about the scheme on the board.
b • Students work in groups preparing their questions. Write them on the board. Students listen and compare.
c • Students listen to Part 3 of the tape and complete the questions.
⊕ • Students say/write full sentences using cues from the tapescript, e.g. *How .... schools .... in the scheme?; How ... money do .... get to start the business?;* They suggest other questions beginning with 'How much/many... ?'
Answer key
How many...sell? How much...make? How many ... team?

3 *Language focus*
How much? How many?
a Look at the examples with the students. Elicit/point out that those words which are/can be written as plurals take *How many*.... Students match the words in the list.
Answer key
How much...?: advice, money, profit, time
How many...?: books, prizes, schools, students
⊕ • Students use the list of words to write complete sentences.
b • Students work together. Provide assistance as necessary.
Answer key
1 How many prizes ...? 2 How many books ...? 3 How much money ...? 4 How much advice...? 5 How much time ...? 6 How much profit ...?

R·W **4** *The Multicolour Glass Company* ⊖
Reading about a woman who has started up her own business and answering comprehension questions.
a • Students look at the photo and try to guess what Mandy's business is. They read the text once through quickly for the answer.
b • Go through the chart with students, before they complete it, explaining vocabulary as necessary, particularly *invested* and *funding*.
 • Check by putting a copy of the chart on the board and completing it with the class.
⊕ • Students find 5 words they would like to know the meaning of and look them up in the dictionary, ask other members of the class or the teacher.
Answer key
type of business: (making) coloured glass
experience: worked in a travel agency
qualifications: a degree in business studies
money invested: £20,000
funding from: themselves, an oil company, an insurance company and a bank
main customers: restaurants, hotels, people with large homes
c • Students discuss other successful businesses or business people that they know about.

S **5** *Discussion* ⊖
Discussing ideas for a business venture.
 • Encourage students to think of things they can do well and enjoy doing.
 • Groups decide on their ideas for a business venture.
 • Students say what each person in the group would contribute and report to the class.

TEACHER'S NOTES

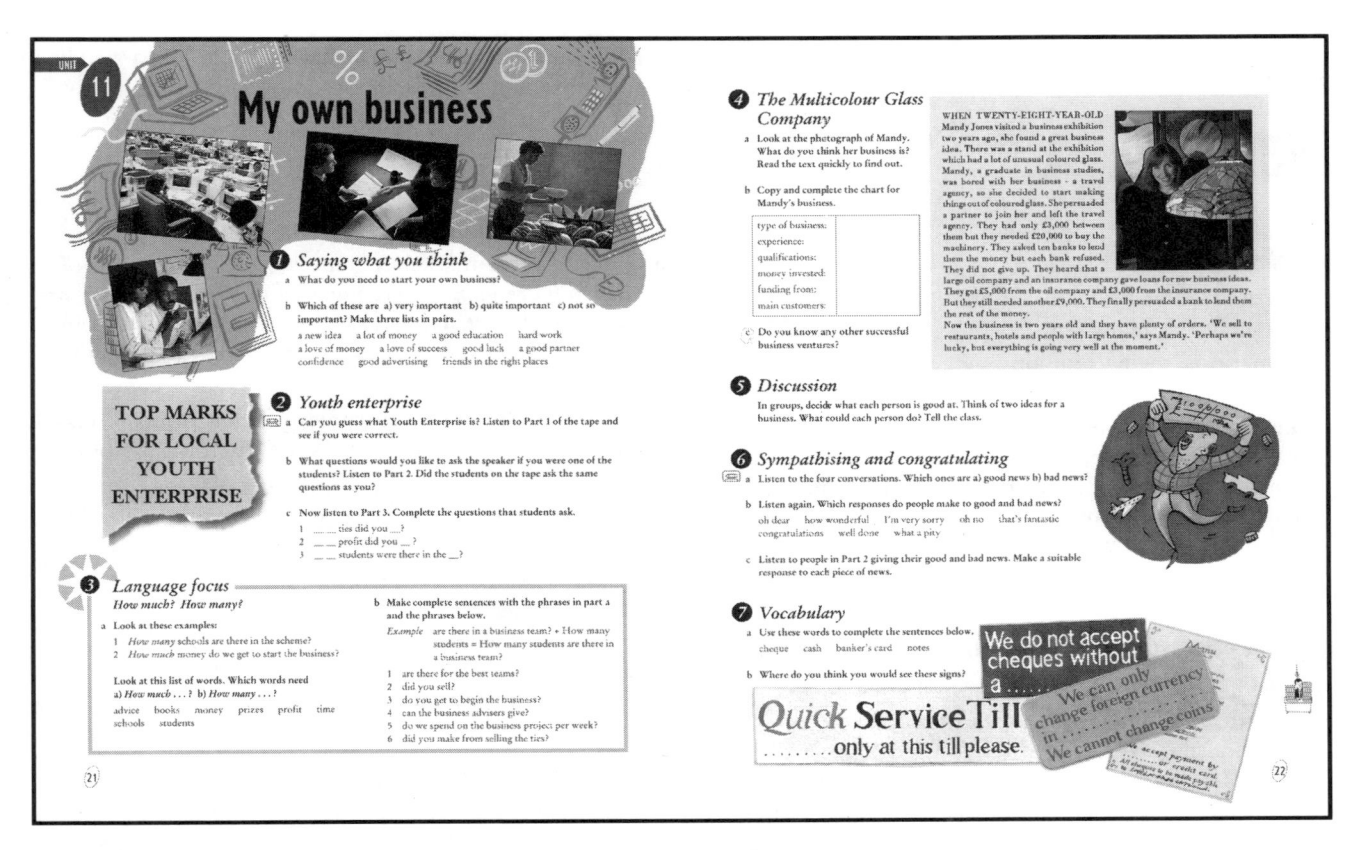

L·W 6 *Sympathising and congratulating*

Listening to short conversations. Focussing on language for responding to good and bad news.

a • Listen to the first conversation. Students tell you if it is a) good or b) bad news. Go through the other 3 conversations in the same way.

Answer key
good news: dialogues B & C; **bad news:** dialogues A & D

b • Make sure students understand that you congratulate someone when they tell you good news and sympathise when their news is bad. Play the tape through, pausing for students to tell you what the responses on the tape to good and bad news are. Write these up on the board under the headings *sympathising* and *congratulating*.

Answer key
responses to good news: That's fantastic! How wonderful! Oh well done. Congratulations!
responses to bad news: Oh dear. I'm very sorry. Oh no. What a pity.

c • Play part 2 of the tape. Ask individual students to respond using the phrases on the board.
⊕ • Replay the tape and get students to repeat the expressions after the speakers. Focus on the correct intonation.

R·W 7 *Vocabulary* ⊖

Words associated with the parts of a cheque and with borrowing money.

a • Allow students to use their dictionaries.
• Students complete the sentences. Ask individual students to read the sentences aloud when checking, and focus on correct stress and pronunciation.

Answer key
cash banker's card notes cheque

b • Students work out where they would see the signs.

Answer key
in a supermarket in a petrol station in a bureau de change on a menu

⊕ • Students draw other signs on the board. The class try to guess where they would see them

Extension activities

1 Numbers
Extra practice on reading and writing numbers, eg 13/30, 101, and of numerical expressions, e.g. 12%, £100.

2 A noughts and crosses game
Write a word on the board, e.g. *time*. Students use the word to produce a correct sentence with *How much...?* or *How many..?* to score their nought or cross.

Teacher's Notes

Unit 12
Marriage

Aims
Structures: *going to* + infinitive for talking about future plans
Functions: giving opinions; agreeing and disagreeing
Lexis: marriage, wedding, tradition, presents, paradise, certificate, video, ceremony, afford, romantic, reception, material, death, funeral, colour, jewellery, bride, bridegroom, equal, abbreviation, album

S **1** *Saying what you think*
Discussing different types of wedding ceremony.

a • Elicit that the photographs are of wedding ceremonies around the world. Go through the vocabulary and the points orally with the students, getting them to tell you as much as they can about the wedding ceremony in their country.
⊕ • Discuss other important ceremonies in students' countries, eg funerals, 'coming of age' ceremonies, graduation, etc.

b • One or two willing students tell the class about their weddings.

R·S **2** *Weddings in paradise*
Reading a jumbled text about alternative weddings and putting the paragraphs in the correct order.

a • Again, discuss this point as far as students are willing.

b • Students give reasons for their answers to the two parts to this question.
• Students put the paragraphs in the correct order. Encourage students to give reasons for the order they have decided on.
⊕ • Put the completed texts on a transparency, so it is easier for the students to see the links between paragraphs.

Answer key
The first text is from a holiday brochure. It is selling alternative weddings. The second text is from a magazine article. It is describing Bob and Carol's wedding plans, but it isn't trying to sell anything.
Correct order: 1: a, c; **2:** d, b

c • Students work together to list advantages and disadvantages. Write their suggestions on the board.

The class can vote on how many would like a wedding like Bob and Carol's/the weddings advertised in the brochures/neither.

3 *Language focus*
Going to + infinitive for future plans.

a • Write some marker sentences on the board: *Carol and Bob are going to get married in Thailand. They are going to fly out.* Underline the verbs and elicit/point out that *going to* in the sentences refers to something they intend to do.

b • Students find more examples of what Bob and Carol are *going to do* in the text. Write them on the board.

c • Students complete the sentences.
⊕ • Students ask a partner 2-3 questions about what they intend doing for their holiday this year. Then they tell the class about their partner's plans.

Answer key
1 ... is going to wear ...   2 ... not going to invite
3 ... he's going to show ...   4 ... going to cost?
5 ... going to stay... 6 ... not going to have ...

L·W **4** *Different traditions* ⊖
Listening to a woman talking about a traditional Indian wedding and answering comprehension questions.

a • Pre-teach *bride* and *bridegroom*.
• Play the tape once through. Use the tape and the photo to establish that Yasmin is Indian and that her wedding will be a traditional Indian wedding.

b • Play the tape again for students to answer the more detailed questions. Encourage the students to use *going to* in their answers to 3 a) - c).

Answer key
1 Red, pink and green.   2 They wear white at funerals.
3 a Her mother's going to make the material into a sari (a traditional Indian dress).   b Her friends are going to paint her hands with henna.   c They're going to buy Yasmin gold before the wedding.

c • Students can discuss this question in pairs and report back to the class. Remind them of points discussed in exercise 1a.

S·W **5** *Opinions*
Class survey on opinions concerning marriage.

• Ask students to read through the questions and make sure they understand them.
• Students move round the class asking 4 or 5 other students and recording their responses.
• One or two students report the results of their survey back to the class.
⊕ • Students write 2 questions of their own on marriage in a similar multiple choice format.

TEACHER'S NOTES

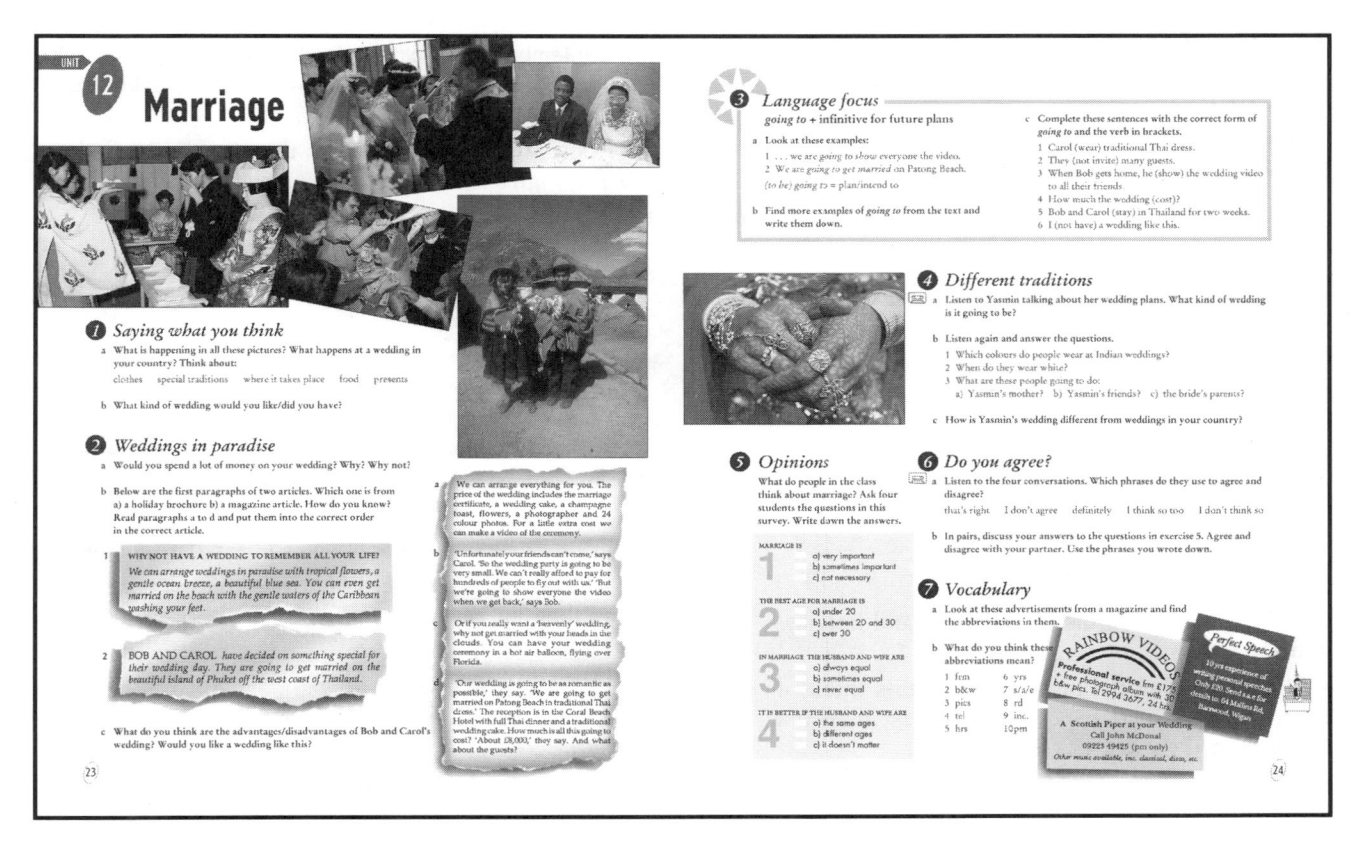

L·W·S 6 *Do you agree?*

Listening to short conversations and focussing on the language of agreement and disagreement.

a • Listen to the first dialogue. Establish that the speakers are talking about marriage.
  • Re-play the first dialogue and play the others, pausing for students to note the language of agreement and disagreement.

  Answer key
  Agree: .. definitely.   I think so, too.   ...that's right.
  Disagree: I disagree.   I don't think so.   No, I don't agree.

b • In pairs, students use the information in exercise 5 to take turns stating their opinions about marriage and agreeing or disagreeing with what their partner has said.

R·W 7 *Vocabulary* ⊖

Understanding abbreviations.

a • Explain the word abbreviation, with examples, eg *USA, EC, UN*.
  • Students identify the abbreviations in the advertisements, but don't ask them to explain them yet.

b • Students work together decoding the abbreviations. Set them a time limit and see who can re-write the most abbreviations within that time.

Answer key
1 from   2 black and white   3 pictures   4 telephone
5 hours   6 years   7 self-addressed envelope   8 Road
9 including   10 afternoons

⊕ • Each student writes 5 abbreviations (in English!) for words or places and gives them to his/her partner to decode.

Extension activities

1 Traditions
Students write 3-4 lines about traditions in their country on certain festival days, or national holidays, for example, New Years day, OR

2 If students are in their home country, they prepare a collage of pictures with short captions showing a ceremony in their country.

3 Crossword
Give students a completed crossword using the key vocabulary from the unit. The students write the clues.

TEACHER'S NOTES

Unit 13
Tips for travellers

Aims
Structures: modals: *must*, *should* and *can*
Functions: giving advice; dealing with money
Lexis: traveller, method, transport, object, mosque, bazaar, bargain, youth hostel, fantastic, book, visa, cotton, passport, boarding card, load, mountainous, cost of living, change money, cash a cheque, credit card, notes, coins

S **① Saying what you think**
Naming different forms of transport and holiday items

a,b • After discussing the questions, students think of other methods of transport and holiday items not featured in the pictures.

c • Discuss types of holiday in general and students' favourites.

L·W **② Experienced travellers**
Listening to people give advice about taking holidays in Egypt, Sweden and Japan and answering comprehension questions.

a • After the students match the countries with the photos, find out if any students have been to these countries.
Answer key
a) Japan - photo B   b) Egypt - photo C   c) Sweden - photo A

b • Play the tape for students to match the conversation to the country.
• To prepare them for the next listening, ask students if they can remember any advice they heard on the tape, but don't dwell on this.
Answer key
a) Japan - C   b) Egypt - A   c) Sweden - B
• See if the students can remember which of the objects in exercise 1 is mentioned. Play the tape, pausing between speakers for students to note down the answers.
• When checking the activity, put the advice from the tape on the board to introduce the Language focus.
Answer key
1 a visa   2 a Go to the bazaars. You should bargain for things.   b Try the Egyptian restaurants and don't eat in the hotel all the time.   c Go in the summer, between May and September.   d You should always book in advance.
e September and October are the best months.   f Take cotton trousers and shirts, a sweater and maybe one jacket.

⊕ • If any students have been to these countries, find out if they agree with the advice on the tape and if they would add to it.

③ Language focus
Must, *should*, *can*.

a • Go through the examples with the students and elicit that *must* is stronger than *should*, ie with *must* there is no choice. Also be sure that students do not confuse this use with the earlier use of *can* to express ability.

b • Students complete the sentences in pairs.
Answer key
1 must   2 can   3 must   4 should   5 must   6 must, can

⊕ • Students write 5 pieces of advice for someone travelling by air, using *must*, *should*, *can*.

R·W **④ Trick cycles** ⊖
Reading a letter and answering comprehension questions.

⊕ • Be sure that students understand that the text was written many years ago, in 1937. Ask them to say or show you on a map where Haiti is. Ask students what they know about Haiti. What do they think is the best way for the traveller to get around Haiti? *NB A trick cycle is the equivalent of a folding bicycle.*
• Students read the text and find the answers to the questions, comparing with a partner.
Answer key
1 Three trick cycles   2 In Haiti   3 They don't weigh much, it is easy to take them to pieces and to pack them, they are strong and carry quite heavy loads, they can travel fast over most types of country, they save hours of walking and can be used to carry heavy shopping and you can carry them comfortably on your back.

⊕ • Students tell the class which is the most convenient means of transport in their country and why.

R·W **⑤ In my country**
Students write and exchange advice for travellers to their country or a country that they know.

• Discuss the categories with students.
• Choose one of the categories and get students to give you pieces of advice for the country in which the lesson is being taught. Elicit advice beginning with *You must ..*, *You should ..*, and *You can ...*
• Students select one or two of the headings and write their advice.
• To make guessing the countries more challenging, the teacher can collect the students' pieces of advice and read them to the class.

TEACHER'S NOTES

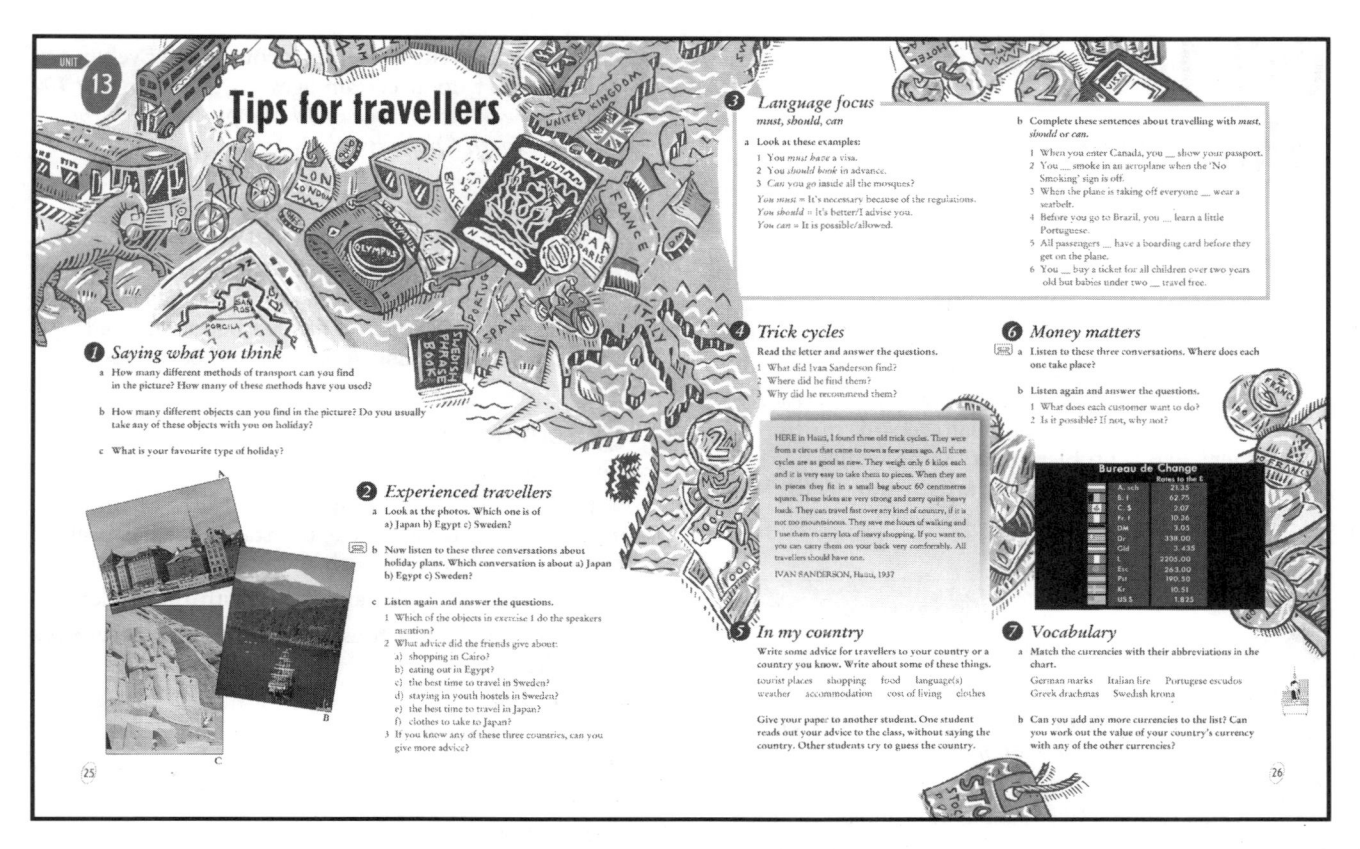

L·S 6 Money matters

Listening to short conversations about money.

a • Students listen to the conversations and say where they take place.

Answer key
Dialogues A and C - in a bank or bureau de change
Dialogue B - in a hotel

b • Check that students understand the concept of exchanging currency and the difference between coins and notes. They will also need to understand the meaning of 'credit card'.
• Students listen and take notes. Pause the tape between dialogues and replay it as necessary.

Answer key
Dialogue A - He wants to buy £1000 worth of traveller's cheques and to change £500 into Hong Kong dollars. Both are possible. **Dialogue B** - She wants to pay by credit card, and it's not possible because the hotel doesn't accept credit cards. Then she asks to cash some traveller's cheques and that is possible. **Dialogue C** - The customer asks to change German marks into pounds. She can change the notes but not the coins.

⊕ • Students roleplay similar conversations in pairs. One or two pairs practise their dialogues for the class.

R·W 7 Vocabulary

Matching the names of currencies with the abbreviations for them. Calculating the value of a currency.

Answer key
German marks = DM, Italian lire = L, Portuguese escudos = Esc, Greek drachmas = Dr, Swedish krona = Kr

a • Students match the currencies with the abbreviations.

b • Students add their own currencies and any more they know to the list.

⊕ • Students take a sum like $10 and each student in the class says what that would equal in his/her own currency.

Extension activities

1 Survey
Find out which countries the people in the class have been to and which one each student liked the best. Find out if there is a 'class favourite'.

2 Word web
Students make a word web with *transport* at the centre.

3 Cost of living chart
Students make a list of items, eg a loaf of bread, a dozen eggs, a pair of jeans, say what they would cost in their country and do a cost of living chart, based on the information. The students should convert all costs into a standard agreed currency to make comparisons.

TEACHER'S NOTES

Unit 14
Whizz kids

> **Aims**
> **Structures:** present perfect simple tense
> **Functions:** checking understanding
> **Lexis:** talent, deaf, autobiography, vibrations, percussionist, orchestra, concert, accept, lip-read, perfect(ly), astonished, musician, record, maths (teacher), extra, problem, (the) same (as), drawing, complex, excellent, artist, strange, to pass an exam, genius, music, art, goals, professional, starred champion

S **1** *Saying what you think*
Discussing special talents and talented people.

a • Explain the meaning of 'talent', ie *the natural ability that someone has to do something well.*

Answer key
Mozart, Greta Garbo, Dalai Lhama, Muhammed Ali, Pele

b • Students discuss the statements in pairs, and then one or two students tell the class what they think.
⊕ • Students suggest other people that have a special talent and say what it is.
⊕ • Suggest other famous people (make sure they are internationally famous). Students tell you what their talent is.

R·W **2** *World class*
Reading an article about an unusually talented musician and answering comprehension questions.

a • Students read the text once through quickly to find out what is unusual about Evelyn. Put their comments on the board. Make sure they understand the meaning of 'deaf' and that she is very talented musician.

Answer key
a She is unusual because 1) she has been deaf since the age of 12 and 2) she has been a very talented musician since she was a child.

b • Students read the text again more slowly and answer the second set of questions. Students compare answers in pairs before the class discuss.
⊕ • Students find 5 words in the text that they would like to know the meaning of and ask the teacher, one another, or look them up in the dictionary.
⊕ • Revision of *can/can't* and *could/couldn't* to describe present and past ability: Students make lists of things Evelyn can and can't do, e.g *She can play the drums. She can't hear.*

Then students write sentences about what Evelyn could/couldn't do at certain ages, e.g *At the age of 10 she could hear. At the age of 14 she played with the National Youth Orchestra.*

Answer key
b 1 She is a percussionist.   2 When she was 14 she played with the National Youth Orchestra of Scotland. When she was 16 she applied to join the Royal Academy of Music.   3 Because she is deaf.   4 She has been deaf since the age of 12.   5 She has learned to lip-read.
6 She can feel the music (going up and down her body).

3 *Language focus*
Present perfect.
Note: The important point about all uses of the present perfect tense is that the statement has present relevance/a connection with the present.

a • Look at the examples and notes with the students.
b • Students decide which use of the present perfect they see in the sentences.

Answer key
a) 1, 3, 5, 6   b) 2, 4

c • Students find other examples of the present perfect in exercise 2.

Answer key
...She has learned to lip-read perfectly... Evelyn has done a lot. She has made several records and she has written **'Good Vibrations'**; 'It has been a wonderful period of my life'; She has learned a lot... She has played...

L·W·S **4** *Talented children* ⊖
Listening to a radio broadcast about two very talented children and answering comprehension questions.

a • Focus students' attention on the photographs of Ricardo and Stephen. Get students to guess their ages and to tell you what they think the boys' talents are.
• Stop the tape after each converstion for students to confirm their guesses about the two boys.

b • Students read the sentences and say whether they apply to Ricardo or to Stephen, before playing the tape.

Answer key
Sentences about Ricardo: 2, 3, 5
Sentences about Stephen: 1, 4, 6,

c • Ask the students to suggest one or two problems and write them on the board. Students then work together and decide on three more problems to report to the class.

S·W **5** *Geniuses?* ⊖
Reading and writing short descriptions of people with special talents.

Teacher's Notes

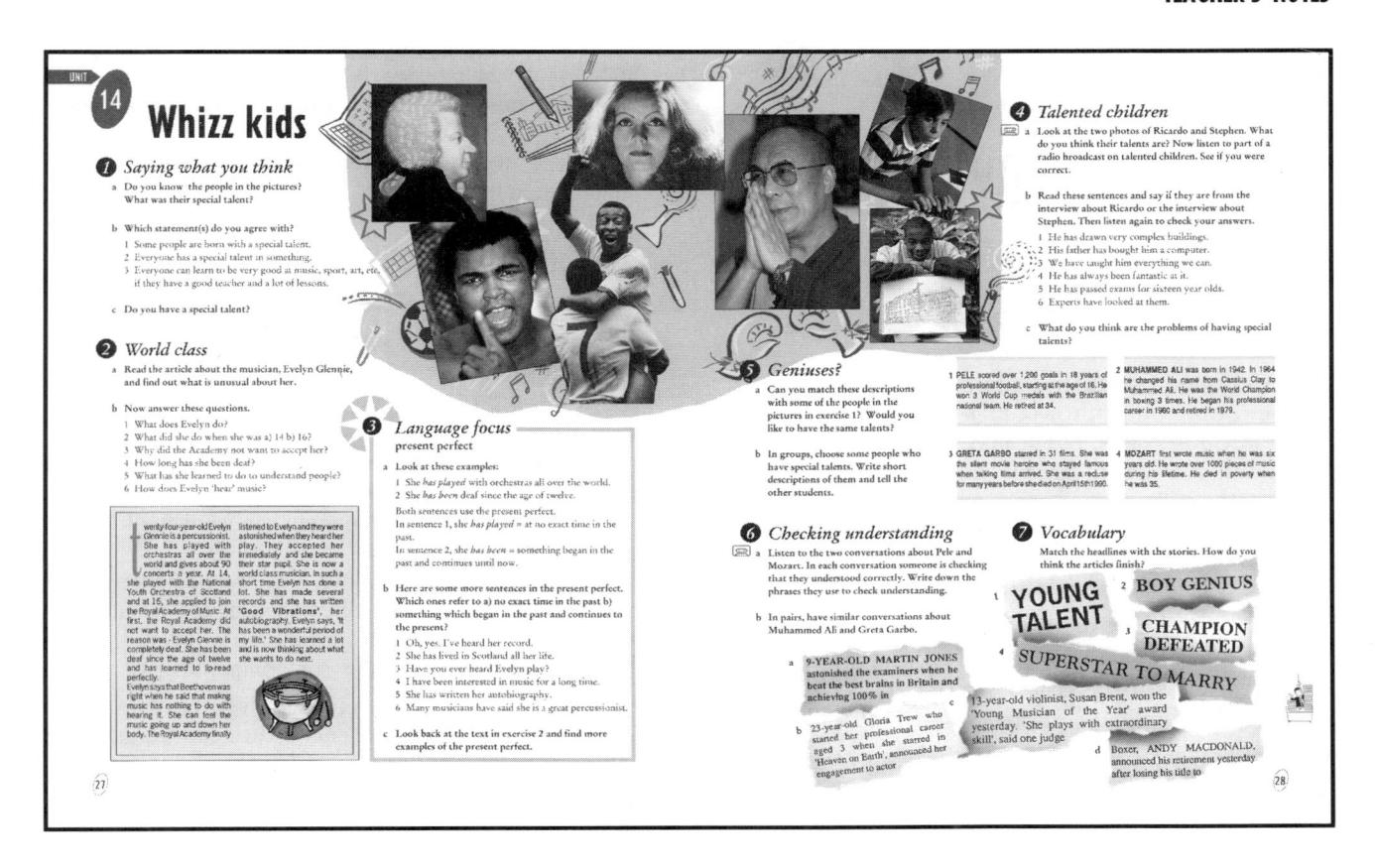

a • Students read the descriptions and match them with the pictures in exercise 1.

⊕ • Students say what special talent they would most like to have and why.

b • In groups, students choose a famous person to write about. If students don't know specific facts or details about the person's life, encourage them to write more generally about the person.

⊕ A spokesperson from each group reads the description aloud but does not give the name of the person. The class has to guess who the person is.

⊕ In groups, students find one other talented person for a selection of categories, eg sport, art, film. Give them a time limit. The group to choose a person for each category first, 'wins'.

L·W·S 6 Checking understanding

Listening to short conversations and focussing on phrases for checking understanding.

a • Students listen and note down the phrases used for checking understanding.

Answer key
What did you say? And let me just check this. Do you mean...?

b • Practise one or two example dialogues yourself with students before you ask them to work in pairs.

• After pair practice, get one or two pairs to act out their conversations for the class.

W 7 Vocabulary ⊖

Matching headlines with news stories and completing the stories.

• Look at and discuss the headlines with the students, before they do the exercise.

• In pairs, students suggest suitable endings for the stories.

⊕ • Students write the endings for the stories.

Extension Activities

1 Headlines
Cut out some headlines from newspaper stories. Students write a story for the headline.

2 Collage
Students do a word and picture collage of a talented/famous person.

3 Profile
Students write a paragraph about someone they admire.

TEACHER'S NOTES

Unit 15
Two's company

Aims
Structures: comparatives and superlatives
Functions: making comparisons
Lexis: twins, personalities, freaks, stare (at), at home, easier, quiet, town, high street, the world, parade, pushchairs, punk, nun, closer, better, festival, more/most famous, normal, identical, properly, pretended, (more) aggressive, noisier, special, together, private, multiple birth, heavy, unusual, high, short, weighed, measured, arrest, tasty, delicious, cheap, refreshing

S **1** *Saying what you think*
General discussion about twins.
⊕ • Before reading, elicit the name of the star sign and any characteristics of Gemini people that students know of.
a • Students read the description of Gemini. If appropriate, they should say whether they agree with it.
b • As a class, students discuss the answers to the questions.
⊕ • Students work together to make a list of facts about twins. E.g. *Some twins look exactly alike and others don't. Twins often have a closer relationship than other brothers and sisters.*

R·W **2** *Freaks*
Reading a text about an unusual town and answering comprehension questions.
a • Before reading, write the name *Twinsburg* on the board and ask students if they can guess what is special about the town. Pre-teach the meaning of *freaks*.
• Students read the text once and answer the questions.
Answer key
1 Ohio, USA. 2 It's a small, quiet town. 3 Once a year, there is a festival for twins.
b • Students discuss the questions in pairs and then give their answers orally. As they give their answers, write the comparative adjectives they use on the board.
Answer key
1 a) In normal life they sometimes feel like freaks. b) In Twinsburg it's easier - they feel at home.
2 a) Twinsburg is usually 'a quiet, little town'. b) At the time of the festival twins come from all around the world and there is a big parade.

3 The relationship between Mark and Mike is closer than it is with other brothers and sisters. They have a better relationship.
4 The festival is bigger, more expensive and more famous than it was in 1976.

3 *Language focus*
Comparative and superlative adjectives.
a • Look at the example and the note with the students. For each question, work with the students to find answers and write 'rules' on the board.
Answer key
1 - if a consonant *(g)* comes after a vowel *(i)*, you double the consonant *(big + g + er)*.
- if the adjective ends in *y (happy)*, the *y* becomes *i* when you add *-er (happier)*
2 You use *-er* with short (1 syllable) and some 2 syllable adjectives. You use *more* with adjectives of 3 syllables or more.
3 The word *than* comes after the comparative form.
b • Students note down the comparative adjectives in the text in Exercise 2. Ask students if they can think of the comparative of *bad*.
Answer key
easier, closer, better, better looking, bigger, busier, more famous. The comparative form of *good* is *better*.
c • Students note down the superlative adjectives in the text in Exercise 2 and decide when to use *est* and *most*, ie., you use *est* with short syllable adjectives and *most* with 3 syllable adjectives.
Answer key
oldest, most expensive, most famous, biggest.
d • Students work together to write sentences using comparative and superlative forms. Write some of their suggestions on the board.
e • Students make sentences using the superlative.
Answer key
Suggested answers: In Twinsburg you can see the *oldest* twins in the world. There are plans to build a museum of the *most famous* ftwins in history. They are planning to build a library for the world's *biggest* collection of information about twins.

L·W·S **4** *Identical twins* ⊖
Listening to an interview with identical twins and answering questions.
a • Tell students they are going to hear an interview with two twins, Martin and Peter. Students discuss the question and tell any stories they may know about twins.
b • Play the tape through for students to listen for the answers to the questions.

TEACHER'S NOTES

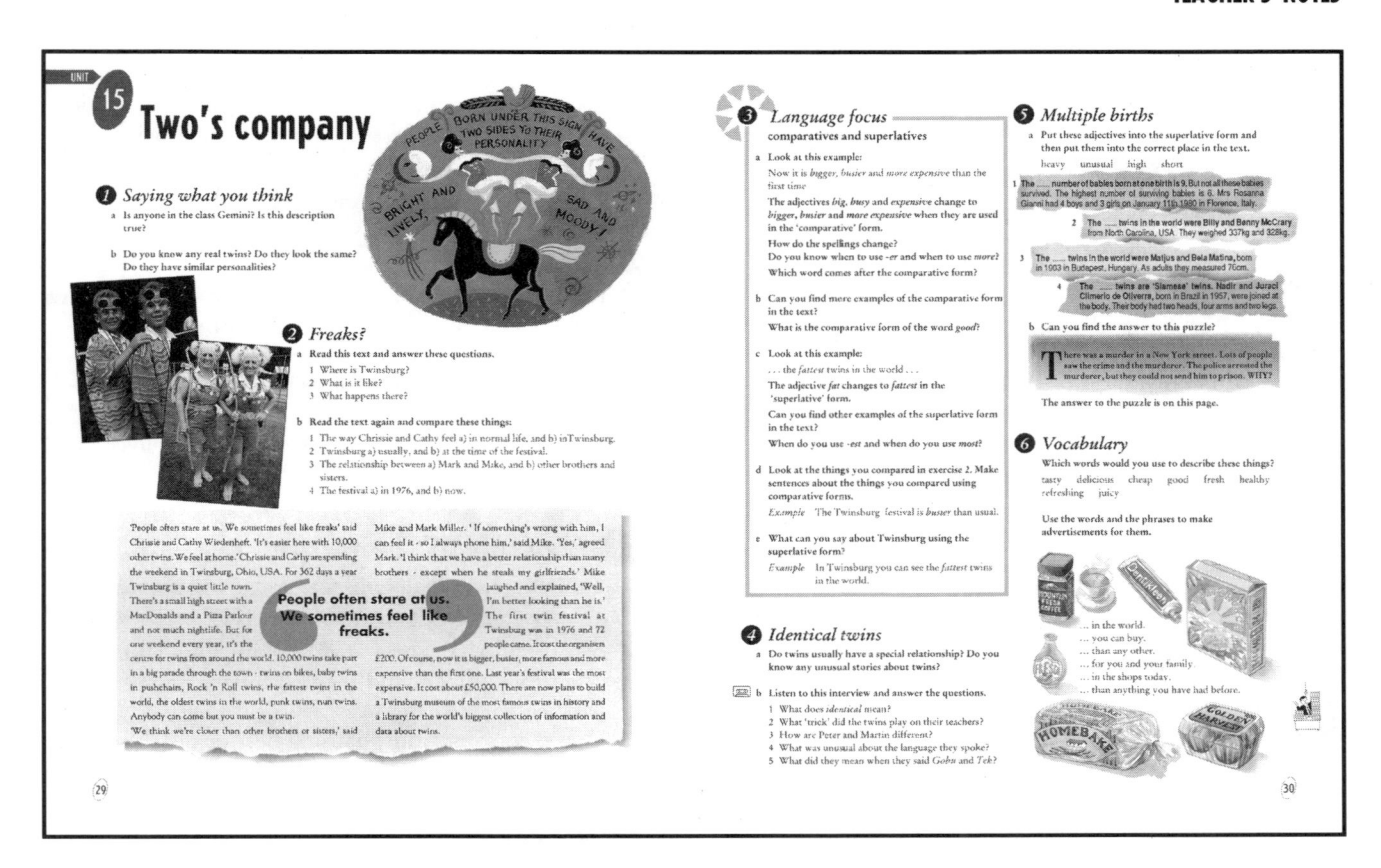

[Page preview of Unit 15 "Two's company" textbook spread]

⊕ • Students try to think of some of the advantages and disadvantages of having a twin brother or sister.

Answer key
1 Identical means exactly the same.
2 They pretended to be one another.
3 Martin is older, more aggressive, noisier.
4 It was only spoken by them.
5 gobu = mum/mummy; tek = no.

R·W·S ❺ *Multiple births*

Practising the use of superlative adjectives. Finding the solution to a puzzle.

a • Students read the texts through and supply the correct superlative adjective. Be sure students understand what is meant by the term 'Siamese' twin, as it is a clue for section b.

Answer key
highest, heaviest, shortest, most unusual

b • Students read through the puzzle. Make sure they understand the vocabulary.
• Students work in groups to find the solution. Tell students to raise their hand when their group thinks it has a solution. OR
Give students a time limit, eg 5 minutes, to find a solution.

⊕ • The activity can be extended if other puzzles of a similar type are readily available.

Answer key
He/they were Siamese Twins. The police could not arrest the killer, without incarcerating the innocent twin.

W ❻ *Vocabulary* ⊖

Using comparative and superlative adjectives to write advertisements.
• Make sure that students understand the vocabulary.
• Complete a couple of phrases as a class as examples.
• In pairs, students write their advertisements.
• Students read their advertisements for the class.

Extension activities

1 Comparisons
Students write, comparing two things they know well, for example, two cities or towns or two people.

2 Advertisement
Students write a short tourist advertisement for their town, using superlative adjectives.
Eg It is the most beautiful town/city in the country/ world.

3 Pairs
Students make a list of things which come in twos, eg shoes, gloves, contact lenses, wings, socks, boots.

TEACHER'S NOTES

Unit 16
What next?

Aims
Structures: *will* and *might* for future certainty and possibility
Functions: making predictions, expressing hopes
Lexis: by hand, floor (of a building) area, offices, mad, storey, shopping precinct, construction company, residents, spokesman, can't stand, heights, possible, certain, working from home, solar energy, housework, robots, predictions, vegetable farm, farming, desert, automatic fishing boats, satellites, raised platforms, salt water, water vapour, domes, plant, pick, pack

S **1** *Saying what you think*
Discussion of how people's lives have changed and how they will change in the future.

a • Suggest events that occurred or life as it was about 200, 100 and 50 years ago and make a list on the board. Ask students for some more suggestions and comparisons.

b • Predict changes in your life in the next 10 and 40 years. Ask students for some suggestions to make a list.

R·W **2** *Aeropolis*
Reading about a city of the future and answering comprehension questions.

⊕ • Before reading, ask students what they think cities will be like in the future. Discuss transport, work, etc.

a • Students read the text and find the answers.
Answer key
1 In the middle of Tokyo Bay   2 2 km   3 25 years
4 In the next four years   5 Individual answers required

b • Students re-read the text to find the answers to the words or phrases. Check their answers, making sure they can pronounce the words correctly.
Answer key
1 has on   2 storey   3 shopping precinct   4 construction company   5 residents   6 spokesman   7 can't stand

⊕ c • In groups, students discuss their predictions. Would they like to live in Aeropolis? Why/why not?

3 *Language focus*
Will and *might*.

⊕ a • Put a sentences with *will* and *might* and the words *certain* and *possible* on the board. Students match the words with the sentences. Underline *will* and *might*
• Look at the examples with the students. Elicit the negative forms of *will* (*won't*) and *might* (*might not*).

b • Complete one of the phrases with the class. Students do the rest in pairs.
Answer key
The construction will be too expensive. **The builders** will not finish it before 2020. **The building** will have 150,000 residents/a secondary school/contain a lot of offices. **The construction company** will build it in Tokyo bay/ need millions of yen.

⊕ • Students write 5 predictions for their own lives in 10 years time, using *will* and *might*.

L·W **4** *Looking to the future*
Listening to short dialogues and focussing on what predictions speakers make and how they express them.

a • Go through the rubric with the students and make sure that they understand the vocabulary and concepts, eg *working from home, solar energy, robots*.
• Play the conversations, pausing between each one for the students to tell you how the speakers feel. Replay each conversation as a check.
Answer key
a) One speaker likes the idea and the other speaker doesn't.
b) They agree that solar energy is a cheap, clean form of energy.
c) They think it's a good idea.

b • Play the tape pausing for students to note the phrases and sentences containing *hope*, *think* and *I don't think so*.
Answer key
Phrases with hope: I hope not. I hope so. I hope we won't have robots to do our jobs as well.
Phrases with think: I think it's quite a good idea to work from home. I don't think so. I think it's the cheapest and cleanest form of energy. I think so too. I don't think so.
Hope and *think* are used in the same way in the positive form, e.g. *I hope/think she will come*. However, they are used differently in the negative, e.g. *I* **hope** *that she will* **not** *come/I* **don't think** *she will come*.

⊕ • Students produce two sentences about each of the topics, using phrases with *hope* and *think*.

W·S **5** *What will happen?*
Writing predictions and telling the class about them.

a • Discuss the categories with the students.
• Focus students attention on the difference between *will* and *might* in the rubric. Choose one of the categories and elicit examples of predictions containing *will* and *might* from the class as a whole, as an example.

Teacher's Notes

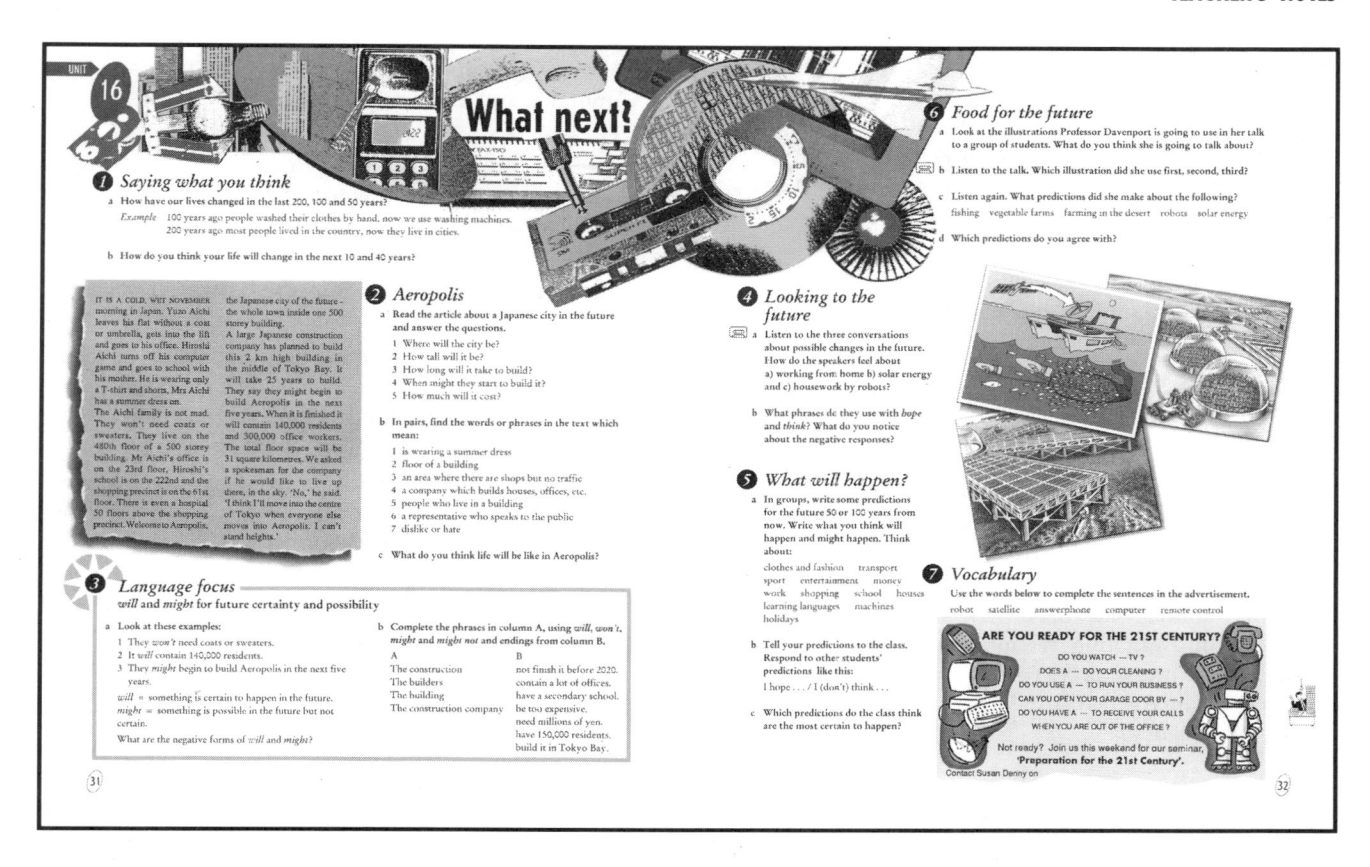

- Students write their predictions in groups. If possible, have them write on a transparency.
- b • Groups read their predictions to the class. Other students respond using phrases with *hope* and *think*.
- c • Class decide on the most likely predictions. Make a list on the board.

L·W·S ⑥ Food for the future ⊖
Listening to a talk and taking notes.

- a • Use the illustrations to pre-teach key vocabulary. Write the students' suggestions on the board.
- b • Students listen to the talk once through and order the illustrations.

Answer key
First: automatic fishing boats. **Second:** vegetable farms. **Third:** farming in the desert.

- c • Play the tape again for students to listen for her predictions. Pause the tape to give students time to write. Allow students to compare what they have written. As a class, students discuss whether they agree with the predictions.

Answer key
1 **fishing:** It will be much better in the future. We might have automatic fishing boats with computers and satellites for telling the boats where to fish. We'll have lots more fish farms.
2 **vegetable farms:** It's possible to have vegetable farms on the sea. They will/might be on raised platforms on the sea. They won't use salt water. They'll use water vapour that comes off the sea as it gets warm.
3 **farming in the desert:** They will grow plants under domes in the desert. 4 **robots:** We might have robots to plant, pick and pack the plants. 5 **solar energy:** We'll have solar energy everywhere in a few years time.

⊕ • Students make their own predictions about what will be done to feed mankind in the future.

W ⑦ Vocabulary ⊖
• Students complete the sentences with the appropriate vocabulary. They discuss the meanings of the words in groups.

Answer key
1 Satellite   2 robot   3 computer   4 remote control
5 answerphone

⊕ • Students make their own definitions for the words. Class vote on the best definition.

Extension activities

1 Tense revision
Students choose one of the topics in section 5a and write 3 paragraphs: (1) describe what it was like 50 years ago, (2) describe it now, and (3) make predictions about what it will be like 50 years from now.

TEACHER'S NOTES

Unit 17
A sense of adventure

> **Aims**
> **Structures:** countable and uncountable nouns: there *is/are* + quantifiers.
> **Functions:** Making complaints and apologies
> **Lexis:** holiday, choice, swimming, hunting, camping, caravans, park, scenery, mountains, valleys, waterfalls, lakes, campsites, hostels, accommodation, villages, luxurious, situated, private, golf course, facilities, water skiing, sailing, windsurfing, scuba diving, fishing, riding, tennis, humidity, beaches, adventurous, travel, agency, animal, scientists, park, tents, river trip, fishing, birdwatching, rafting, map, camp, riverside, (in a) mess, dirty, spider, washbasin, sand, peaceful, uncrowded, trekking, foot hills, optional, sights

S **1** *Saying what you think*
Discussing holidays and holiday photographs.
⊕ • Bring in your own holiday photographs and ask students to guess where the places are.
a • Discuss the photographs and questions. Ask students where they think these places are and what kind of holiday they offer.
b • Students ask you the questions first, and then you ask one or two of the students.
• Students work together asking and answering the questions.

R·S **2** *Holiday choice*
Reading about different holidays, matching them with photographs, and discussing their positive and negative points.
a • Students read the texts and match them to the photographs. Allow students to use their dictionaries but encourage them not to try to understand every word.
Answer key
1 Aigues Tortes National Park 3 Mauritius
b • In pairs, students list the positive and negative points of the holidays. They will obviously be subjective and will reflect their own preferences.

3 *Language focus*
Countable and uncountable nouns.
⊕ • Look at the table with the students. Ask them why there is no plural of 'scenery'. Provide further examples from exercise 2 for a table on the board. Ask students in groups to write their own grammar note and 3 more examples of countable and uncountable nouns.
a • Students put the words into the correct column.
Answer key
Countable nouns: cars, caravans, mountains, valleys, waterfalls, lakes, hostels, sports facilities, crowds.
Uncountable nouns: fish, fruit, accommodation, humidity, traffic, entertainment, camping
b • Look at the example with the students and ask them why *some* is used. Write further sentences on the board with the students, using the other chart headings. Students write sentences in pairs.

L·S **4** *Adventurous ideas* ⊖
Listening to an interview with a travel agent and answering questions.
⊕ • A map of the world and some travel/unusual holiday brochures would be useful realia for this activity.
⊕ • Ask students to locate the countries in exercise 1 on the map. Let them look at the travel brochures.
a • Students listen to the tape and tick/note the places the travel agent mentions.
Answer key
The travel agent mentions: Britain, Belgium, France, Spain, Switzerland, Zambia, Sweden
She arranges holidays in: Zambia, France, Sweden
b • Students write headings: *Zambia, France, Sweden*. They listen to the tape and write the relevant activities under the correct heading.
⊕ • Alternatively, write the activities on the board, pre-teach them and then have students listen to the tape and match the holidays with the places, ie, Zambia, France, Sweden
• Students in groups say whether they would like to go on any of these activities, giving reasons.
⊕ • Students choose a holiday from the brochure and give reasons for their choice.
Answer key
Zambia: stay in an animal conservation park; watch the scientists; walks, fishing trips, birdwatching trips.
France: hot-air ballooning.
Sweden: rafting, camp on the riverside.

S **5** *Guesswork* ⊖
Guessing game about holiday destinations.
• Can be done as a group or class activity.
• Get students to suggest possible questions and write a list on the board.

TEACHER'S NOTES

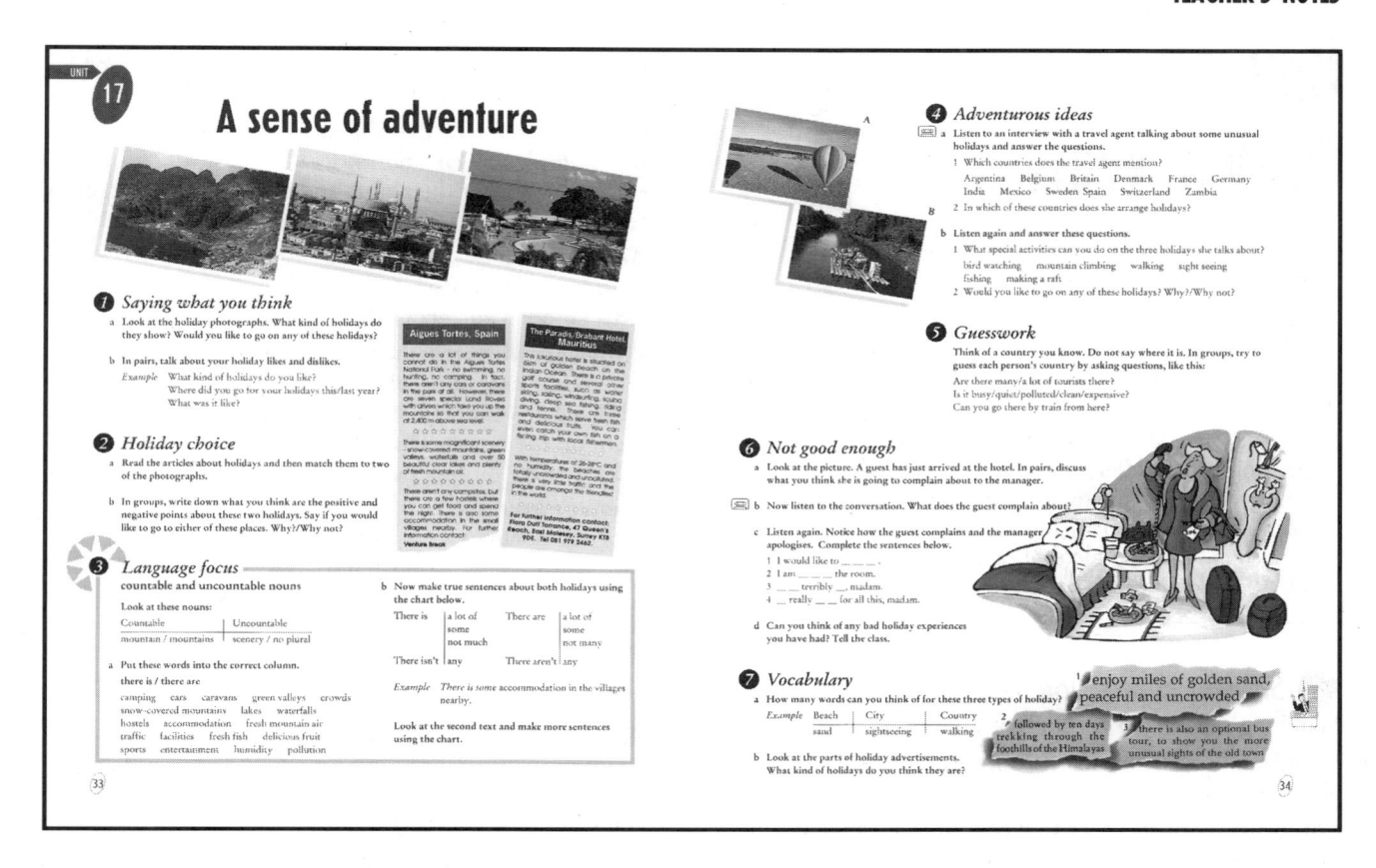

UNIT 17 — A sense of adventure

• Think of a country yourself and get students to ask you questions as an example.

L·S 6 Not good enough

Listening to a conversation and focussing on language of complaint and apology.

a,b • Students use the illustration to predict the woman's complaints. Focus on key vocabulary. Alternatively, students can write a list of complaints before they listen and use the tape to check their predictions.

c • Students listen to the tape and complete the sentences.

Answer key
1 ...make a complaint   2 I am not satisfied with...
3 I am...sorry   4 I ... must apologise.

d • Students discuss bad holiday experiences.
⊕ • Students do a similar guided roleplay, eg complaining about food in a restaurant.

R·S 7 Vocabulary ⊖

Producing holiday related vocabulary and identifying types of holiday in advertisements.

a • Students can work together. You could give them a time limit, eg five minutes, and see which group can produce the most words in that time.

b • Students identify the type of holiday.
⊕ • Students suggest other types of holiday, eg *a coach holiday, a skiing holiday*

Answer key
country holiday; beach holiday; city holiday

Extension activities

1 Holiday description
Students describe the last holiday they took. Should be guided. Useful for revision of holiday vocabulary and past tenses.

2 Collage/advertisement
Students compile pictures with captions to show the best features of their country.

3 Talk
Students give a short talk about their country or about the most interesting country they have been to.

TEACHER'S NOTES

Unit 18
Golden years

Aims
Structures: present perfect tense with *for* and *since*
Functions: offering, accepting and refusing help; talking about experiences
Lexis: youngish, infant, middle-aged, elderly, pension(er), toddler, honeymoon, grandchildren, college, nursing/nurse, a (big) help, (fifty) odd years, sick, horseman, retired, (a) long life, gambling, climate, alcohol, a seat, to manage, OAP, widow, widower

S ### 1 *Saying what you think*
Matching age-related vocabulary to photographs.
a • Students match the words/phrases with the photographs.
b • Students work together to write three advantages and three disadvantages of being old.
• Put students' responses on the board. Did they list more advantages or disadvantages?
⊕ • Students suggest the advantages and disadvantages of being a teenager, a baby, an adult, etc.

L·W ### 2 *In the family*
Listening to conversations and completing sentences containing *for* and *since*.
a • Students listen to each conversation once and match it with the appropriate photograph.
Answer key
Part 1 - couple,   Part 2 - two women and children,
Part 3 - old man
⊕ • Students try to complete the sentences before they listen to the tape.
b • Play the tape as many times as necessary for students to fill in the blanks.
Answer key
1 've been ... for ...   2 ... has been ... since ...
3 ... haven't ... since ... went...   4 've lived ... then.
5 have changed ... stopped.   6 ... for fifty ...
7 ... twenty years.

3 *Language focus*
Present perfect tense with *for* and *since*.
a • If necessary, use a simple timeline to reinforce the idea that *since* is used with a point in time and *for* is used with a period of time.
b • Students refer to the sentences in section 2 and find the examples of *for* and *since*.
• Elicit/point out the points and periods of time in each sentence in exercise 2.
Answer key
with for: 3 sentences, 1, 6 and 7;
with since: 4 sentences, 2 ,3 , 4 and 5.
c • Students work together to put *for* or *since* in front of the appropriate time phrase.
• Elicit 3 or 4 example sentences from the class and write them on the board. Then students write 3-4 sentences individually.
Answer key
1 for six months   2 for five years   3 since 1988
4 for a few hours   5 since 6 o'clock   6 since last week
7 for ten weeks   8 for a long time   9 for years
10 since I got married   11 since he started work
12 for about five days

R·W·S ### 4 *Over a century* ⊖
Reading a text about a man who is 103 years old and answering questions. Discussing what you should do if you want to live to be 100.
⊕ • Discuss the photo of Sid Wright briefly. Ask students how old they think he is.
a • Students read the text and find out why he's in the news. Which students guessed his age the most closely?
b • Students read the text again and put the sentences about Sid in the correct order.
Answer key
He became a horseman. His son George was born. He retired. He came to live with George and Joyce. He started to give interviews on the radio. He had his 103rd birthday.
c • Choose one of the categories and write suggestions as a class. The suggestions begin: *You should/shouldn't*.
• Each group chooses their category before starting to write so the suggestions don't overlap.
• Each group writes 3-4 sentences.
• Groups read their suggestions aloud to the class. Class votes on the best suggestions.

L·W ### 5 *A helping hand*
Listening to short conversations and focussing on language for offering, accepting and refusing help.
a • Students listen to the conversations and suggest where each one takes place.
Answer key
1: on a bus;   2: in the street;   3: in a supermarket

Teacher's Notes

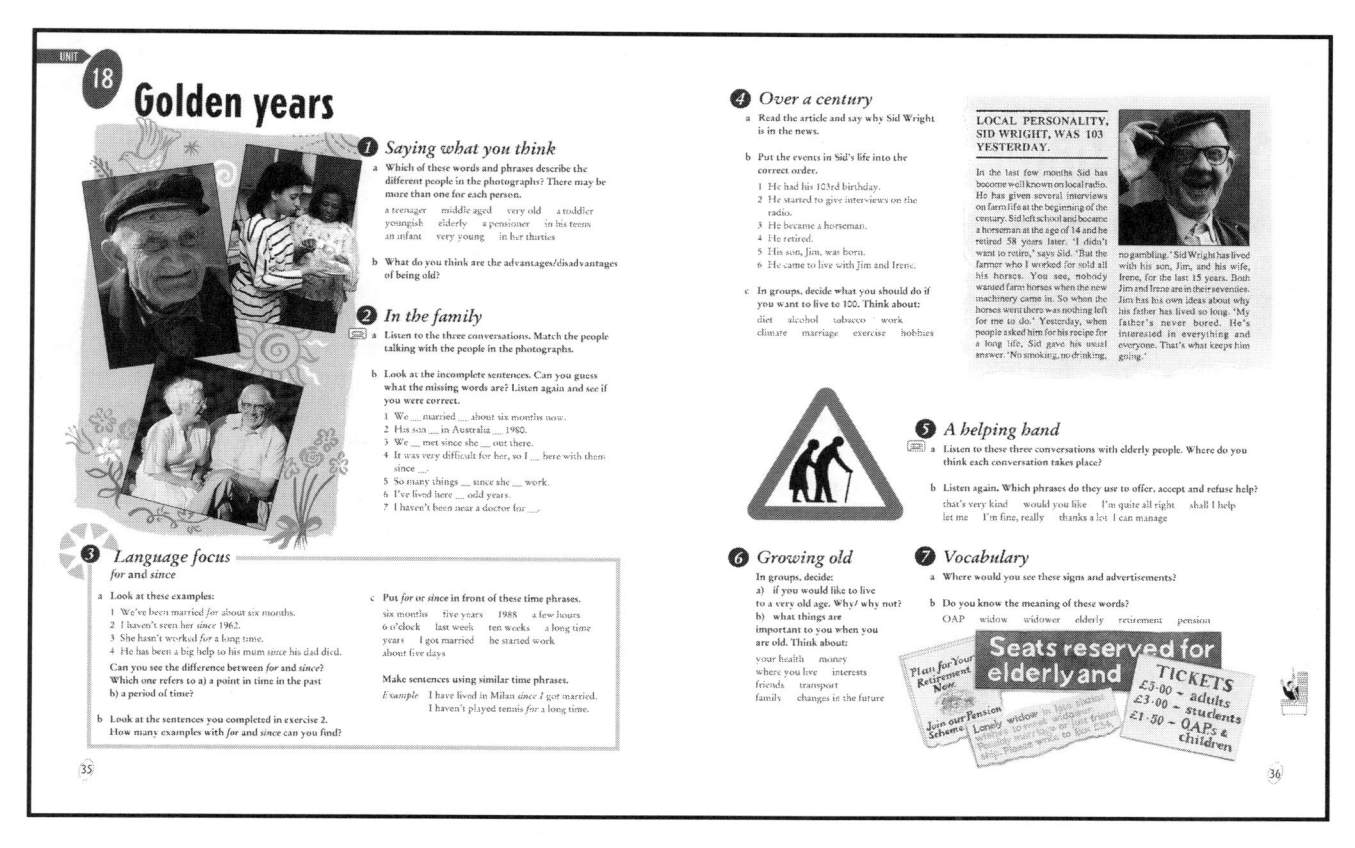

Unit 18 — Golden years

b • Write *offer*, *accept*, *refuse* as headings on the board. Students listen again and suggest phrases from the list to go under the headings.

Answer key
Offer: would you like   let me   shall I help
Accept: that's very kind   thanks a lot.
Refuse: I'm quite all right.   I'm fine, really.   I can manage

⊕ • Set up practice roleplay situations which parallel those in the dialogues. Students practise in pairs. One or two pairs practise their dialogue for the class.

S ⑥ Growing old ⊖

Discussing what kind of life you would like if you were very old.

a • Students decide if they would like to live to an old age and give reasons for their decisions.

b • Go through the categories with students and ensure they understand them.
• Introduce 'I would like to have/be/do ..'. Groups should try to write at least one sentence for each of the categories.

⊕ • Groups can pass on their work to another group for correction.

⊕ • Each group reads their ideas for one or two of the categories. The other groups listen and say if they agree or disagree.

W ⑦ Vocabulary ⊖

Words and phrases associated with old age.

a • Students suggest places where they might see each of the signs.

Answer key
at a bank/building society; on a bus/train; in a newspaper; at a cinema

b • Students work together to discuss and find the meaning of the vocabulary items. Encourage them to use their dictionaries. NB OAP = Old Age Pensioner.

Extension activities

1 Interview
Students think of/imagine someone they know who is over 60, for example, a grandparent. They write 5 questions they would like to ask that person about what it is like to be that age.

2 Word web
Students write a word web with the word *age* in the centre.

3 Hobbies
Students list 5 hobbies/pastimes. They write sentences with for/since to say how long they have enjoyed doing those things. *I have enjoyed learning English for two years/since 1986.*

TEACHER'S NOTES

Unit 19
Fun and games

Aims
Structures: *must*, *have to* and negative forms *must not* and *do not have to*
Functions: describing rules, persuading and conceding
Lexis: chess, draughts, game, play/player, dice, a (games) board, (a handful of) beans, corner, continue, rules, correct, square, pieces, buttons, bottom, top, other side, diagonally, backwards, forwards, waist, gloves, referee, win/winner, cheat, shuffle, matches

S ❶ *Saying what you think*
Discussing different types of games.

a • Use the illustrations to elicit key vocabulary, eg dice, *(a pack of) cards*, etc.
• Students identify these games and any others they know the names of. If students don't know the name in English, encourage them to mime or draw it so that you or the other students can guess it's name.
Answer key
chess, draughts, crossword, cards, scrabble

b • Find out what sort of games are popular in students' home countries, eg board games, card games, games with dice, etc.

R·W·S ❷ *Playing the game*
Reading rules for two games and answering comprehension questions. Explaining the rules of a game.

a • Find out if any students in your class have ever played either of these games.
• Students read the texts once and match the games with the pictures.
Answer key
Picture 1 - Chicago   **Picture 2** - Fan Tan

b • Students will need to read the texts carefully to answer these questions.
• Students can compare answers to T/F questions in pairs before a class check.
Answer key
1f 2f 3t 4t 5f 6f 7t 8f

⊕ • Students work in pairs. Each student writes 2-3 true/false questions of their own on either of the games. His/her partner tries to answer them without referring to the text.

c • Students explain the rules of Chicago to their partner. Then one or two students can explain the rules to the class.
⊕ • Students explain the rules of a game they play at home to their partner.

❸ *Language focus*
Have to, do not have to, must, must not.

a • Look at the examples with the students. Students should see that *have/has to* expresses obligation. (In this case, obligation is expressed within the context of the rules of the game.)
• Students find other examples of *have/has to* in the texts.
Answer key
... have to score 3 ... they have to get a 4 ... someone has to write down the scores ... you don't have to buy ... the banker has to give each player 5 beans ... have to put one of their beans ... have to give theirs to the banker.

b • Look at the examples with the students and ask them to match them with the appropriate meaning.
• Students find another example of *do not have to* and *must not* in the texts. Write them up on the board under the headings *not necessary* and *not allowed*.
Note: The concept of choice might be a useful one if students are having difficulty understanding the contract between *must not* and *don't have to*, ie with *don't have to* there is a choice or alternative, whereas with *must not* there is not.
Answer key
don't have to = not necessary, must not = not allowed
... the players *must not* throw ... you don't have to buy ...

L·W ❹ *Five Field Kono* ⊖
Listening to the rules of a game explained. Using notes to describe the rules and then playing the game.

a • Write a square up in the board and demonstrate/elicit key vocabulary of direction and location, eg *forwards, backwards, diagonally, top, bottom, corner*, etc..
• Play the tape through once for students to identify the correct board, *board c*.

b • Play the tape as many times as necessary for students to describe the rules of the game.
• Students can use the tapescript for a final check of what they have written.

c • Students will need to prepare a board before they play the game in pairs.
• Students should try to say why it is better to move/not move first.

Teacher's Notes

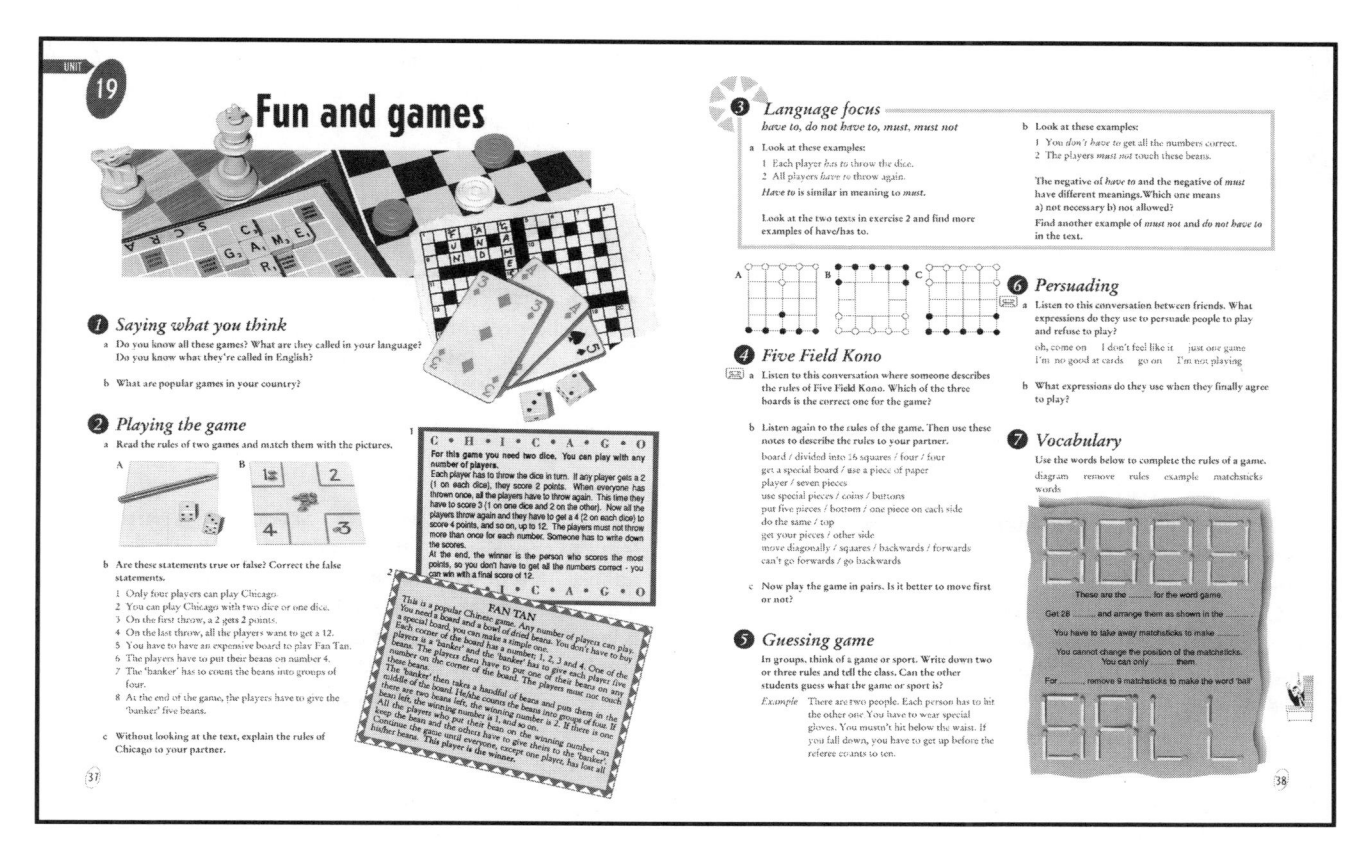

S ⑤ Guessing game ⊖

Writing the rules for a game or sport so other students can guess what it is.

a • Go through the rules for the sport with the class and get them to tell you which sport it is (boxing).

⊕ • Read the rules for a sport that you know to the class and get them to guess which sport it is.
• Students work together writing their rules. Circulate, helping students to prepare their rules.
• Each group/pair reads their rules aloud to the class.

⊕ • 20 questions: Students think of a game or sport and write it down. The other students can ask up to 20 yes/no questions to find out what it is.

L·W ⑥ Persuading

Focussing on language for persuading someone to do something and refusing or agreeing to be persuaded.

a • Students listen and note/tick the expressions as they hear them.

Answer key
Persuading: oh come on   just one game   go on
Refusing: I don't feel like it   I'm no good at cards   I'm not playing

b • First, see if students remember the expressions from memory. Then play the tape for them to check.

Answer key
Go, on then, we'll play. But just one game.

S·R ⑦ Vocabulary ⊖

⊕ • Bring a box of matches to class.

a • Students work in pairs to complete the rules. If you like, the first pair to complete them can be given a small prize.

Answer key
rules   matchsticks   words   remove   example

⊕ • Other commercial word games like Boggle or Scrabble can also be useful for extending students' vocabulary.

Extension activities

1 Invent a game
Students in groups invent their own game and write rules for it.

2 Instructions
Students write the instructions for playing a simple game that they already know.

3 Guess the game
Students write the names of 10 items associated with a game or sport, eg, *pawn*, *puck*. Then they give the list to their partner who tries to supply the name of the game or sport.

TEACHER'S NOTES

Unit 20
Animal facts

Aims
Structures: first conditional
Functions: expressing fear and dislikes
Lexis: afraid, pet, zoo, smelly/smelliest, zorilla, release, liquid, zebra, lions, piranha (fish), extremely, injured, creature, attack, (to be) lost, poisonous, spider, to leave alone, bother, disturb, bite, characteristics, cat, parrot, shark, crab, snake, cockroach, purr, hide. rocks, come near, octopus, lobster, close up, pick up, to change colour, in/out of danger, to match, surroundings, attacker, rubbery, shoot off, cloud, female, lay, egg, guard, hatch, train, temperament, stamina, size, calm, crowds, obedient, mix with, fear, frightening, cage

S **① Saying what you think**
Discussing different/favourite animals.
a • Ask students to name some/all of the animals in the illustration.
• Students say which animals they are afraid of/which are their favourites and why.
b • Discuss the questions. Encourage students to give reasons for their opinions.

R·W **② Amazing animals**
Reading short texts about unusual animals. Discussing the special characteristics of each of the animals.
a • Students read the text through and choose the correct last line for each one, before matching them with the the illustrations in exercise 1.
Answer key
1 4   2 2   3 1   4 3
b • Students decide if the statements are true or false.
Answer key
1 F   2 F   3 F   4 T
c • Explain that almost every animal has a special characteristic, e.g. cats can see very well in the dark, bats cannot see at all, etc. Can students think of any more animals?
⊕ • Students describe an unusual/interesting animal to their partner and their partner guesses the name of the animal.
Answer key
1 The zorilla is the smelliest animal in the world.

2 Piranha fish will attack any injured creature they smell.
3 Many dogs have an excellent sense of direction.
4 The Brazilian wandering spider is the most poisonous spider in the world.

③ Language focus
First conditional.
a • Look at the examples with the students. Focus on the use of the present simple tense in the 'if-clause' and the future simple tense in the main clause of each sentence. Also point out the comma which separates the clauses.
b • Allow students to use their dictionaries for this exercise.
Answer key
If you stroke a cat, it will purr.   If you train a parrot, it will learn to speak.   If a shark smells blood, it will prepare to attack.   If a dog gets lost, it will try to find its way home. If a crab is in danger, it will hide between the rocks.
If you don't disturb a snake, it won't bite you.   If a lion smells a zorilla, it won't come near.   If a cockroach touches a human, it will clean itself.

L·W **④ Sea zoo** ⊖
Listening to an interview about sea animals and answering comprehension questions.
a • Students identify the three creatures in the illustration. Have students ever seen one of these animals live? Up close?
b • Explain that a sea zoo is like any other zoo, but it is a place for keeping sea/marine animals. Find out if students have ever been to a sea zoo.
• Play the tape once straight through and then play it in sections. Allow students to compare their answers in pairs between playings of the tape.
Answer key
1 If they don't live near the sea, they can come and see and even touch sea creatures and plants.
2 Sharks, because they're usually afraid of them, and lobsters, because they can pick them up and because they're strange-looking creatures.
3 It will shoot off and release a black liquid which contains a chemical with a strong smell.
4 When the eggs hatch she will die.

R·W·S **⑤ Working dogs** ⊖
Reading an extract about guide dogs for the blind and answering comprehension and discussion questions.
a • Elicit suggestions for the types of work that dogs do, eg *guard dogs*, *sniffer dogs* (for drugs). Students read the text and answer the question.
Answer key
The dogs are trained to guide/lead blind people.

Teacher's Notes

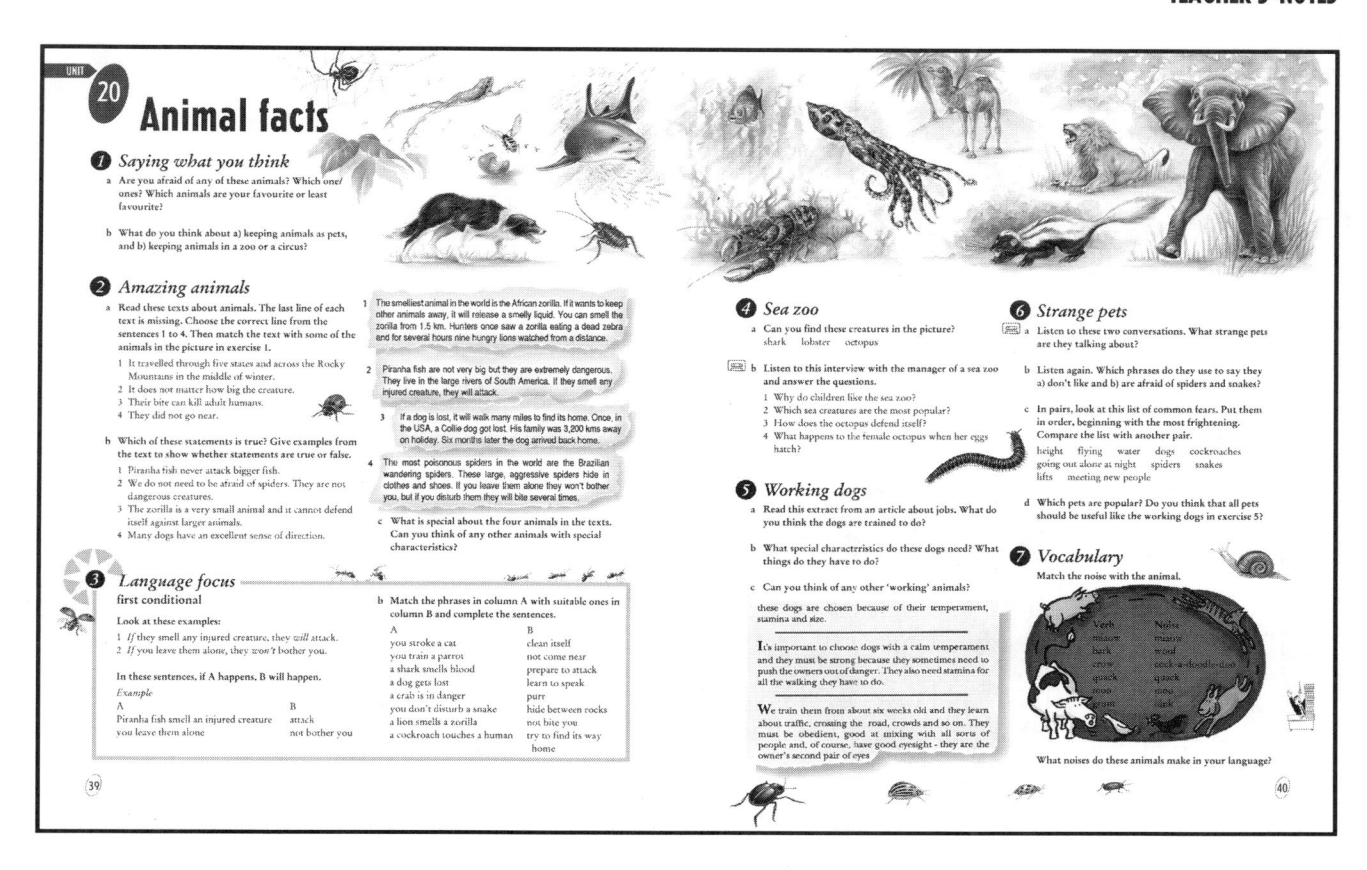

b • Students read the text again and note down the special characteristics the dogs need and what they have to do.

Answer key
1 They must have a calm temperament, stamina and be the right size. They must be strong. They must be obedient, good at mixing with people, and they must have good eyesight.
2 **Suggestions:** They have to keep their owners out of danger. They have to cross roads and go through crowds.

c • Students discuss the answer to this question as a class.

⊕ • Class discuss the expression *A dog is a man's best friend*. Why do we say this? Do students think it is true?

L·W·S ⑥ *Strange pets*

Focus on language for expressing fears. Students discuss their own fears.

⊕ a • Ask students for kinds of animals that people keep as pets. Encourage them to suggest unusual pets as well as cats, dogs, etc.

Answer key
spiders and snakes

b • Students listen again and note the phrases the speakers use.

Answer key
Expressing dislike: I can't stand.... **Expressing fear**: I'm terrified of it/them. I'm scared of...

c • Elicit what the students in the class are most frightened of and put their answers on the board. Compare their answers with the list of common fears in the book.
• Students order the items and compare their lists with a partner's.

⊕ • Students describe a frightening experience they have had.

⑦ *Vocabulary* ⊖

• Students suggest which animal makes which noise. They then write the corresponding noise in their language.

Answer key
miaow - cat   woof - dog   cock-a-doodle-doo - cockerel
quack - duck   moo - cow   oink - pig

Extension activities
1 Profile
Students choose an animal and write a paragraph describing an interesting feature of it, eg its appearance.
2 Class survey
Students find out what pets are the most popular amongst students in the class.

KEY TO PRACTICE SECTION

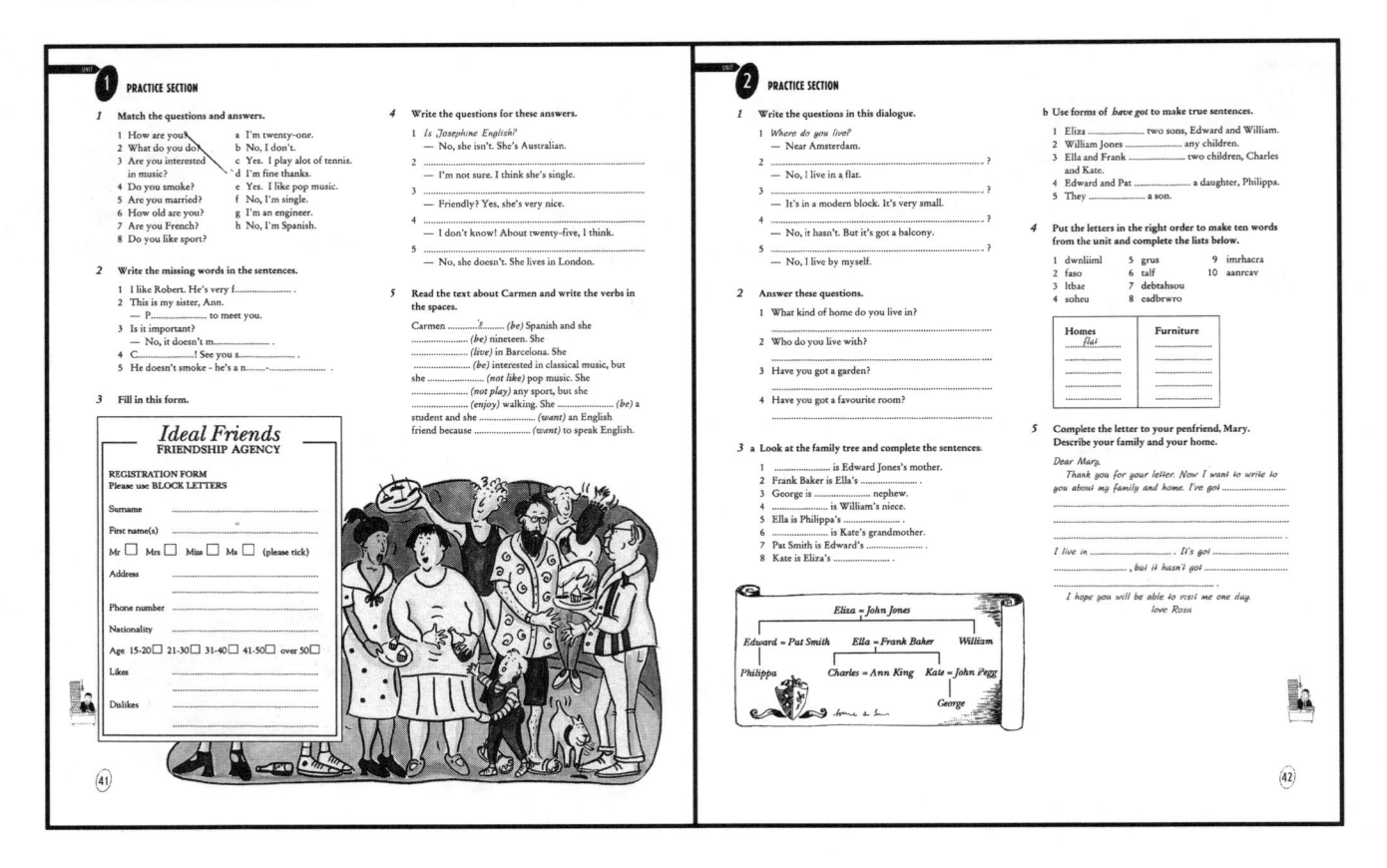

Unit 1

1   2g   3e   4b   5f   6a   7h   8c

2   1 funny   2 Pleased   3 matter   4 Cheerio! ... soon
    5 non-smoker

3   Individual answers required.

4   2 Is she married?   3 Is she friendly?
    4 How old is she?   5 Does she live in Paris?

5   *is* nineteen   *lives* in Barcelona   *is* interested
    doesn't like pop music   *doesn't play* any sport
    enjoys walking   *is* a student   *wants* an English friend
    wants to speak ...

Unit 2

1   2 Do you live in a house?   3 What's it like?
    4 Has it got a garden?   5 Do you live with anyone else?

2   Individual answers required.

3 a   1 Eliza ...   2 ... husband   3 ...Charles'   4 Kate ...
      5 ... aunt   6 Eliza ...   7 ...wife   8 ... granddaughter

  b   1 has got   2 hasn't got   3 have got   4 have got
      5 have got

4   **Homes:** windmill, house, flat, houseboat, caravan
    Furniture: sofa, table, rugs, wardrobe, armchair

5   Individual answers required.

KEY TO PRACTICE SECTION

Unit 3

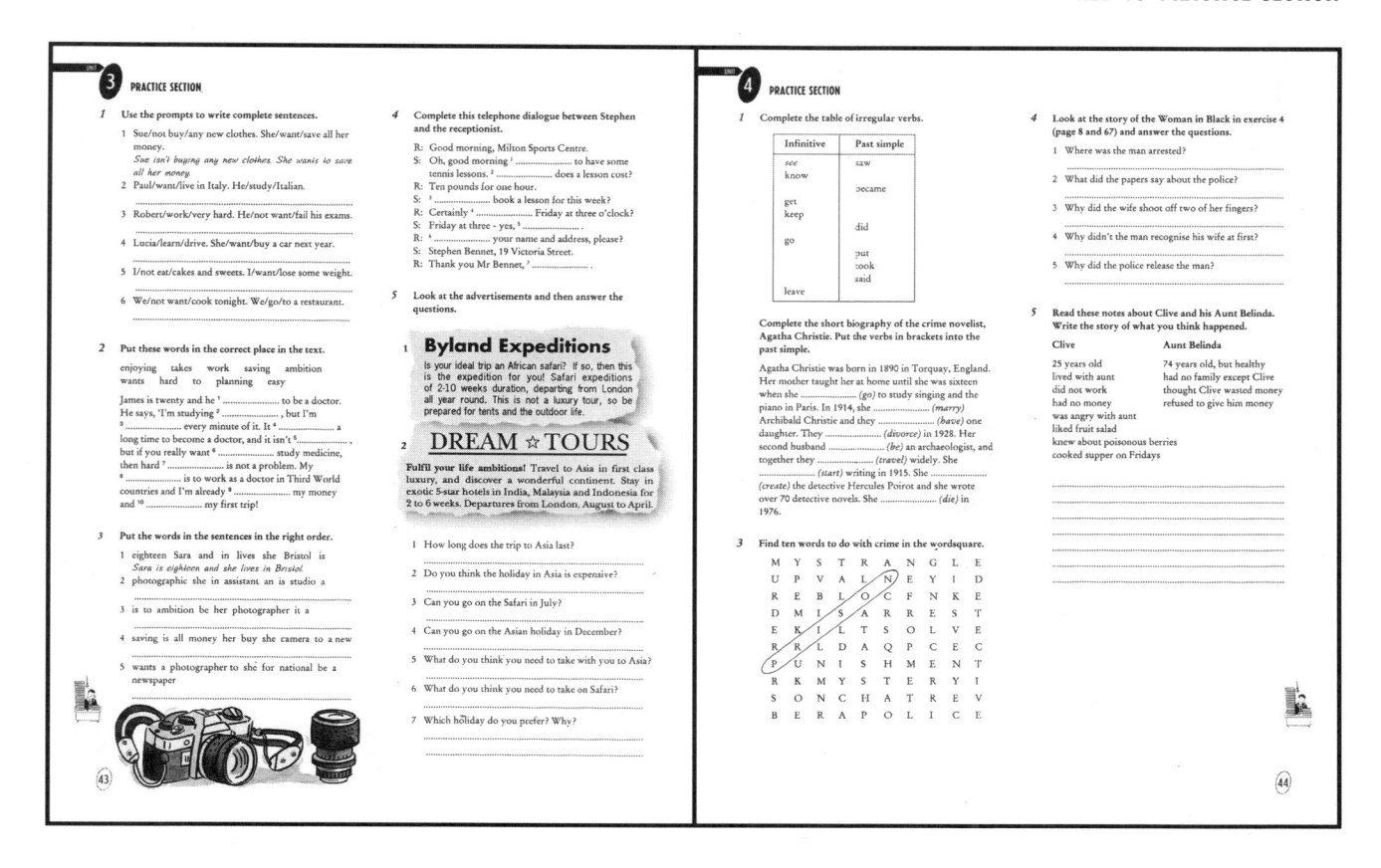

1 2 Paul wants to live in Italy. He's studying Italian.
3 Robert is working very hard. He doesn't want to fail his exams.
4 Lucia is learning to drive. She wants to buy a car next year.
5 I'm not eating cakes and sweets. I want to lose some weight.
6 We don't want to cook tonight. We're going to a restaurant.

2 1 wants 2 hard 3 enjoying 4 takes 5 easy 6 to
7 work 8 ambition 9 saving 10 planning

3 2 She is an assistant in a photographic studio.
3 It is her ambition to be a photographer.
4 She is saving all her money to buy a new camera.
5 She wants to be a photographer for a national newspaper.

4 1 I want ... 2 How much ...? 3 Can I ...?
4 How about ...? 5 ... that's fine 6 ...Could I have ...?
7 ...Goodbye.

5 1 It lasts 2-6 weeks.
2 Individual answers required.
3 Yes, you can.
4 Yes, you can.
5, 6, 7 Individual answers required.

Unit 4

1 new become got kept do went put take
say left

2 *went* to study *married* Archibald Christie *had* one daughter *divorced* in 1928 *was* an archaeologist *travelled* widely *started* writing *created* Hercule Poirot *died* in 1976

3 **Across:** strangle, arrest, solve, punishment mystery, police
Down: murder, detective
Diagonally: kill, prison

4 1 He was arrested on a train to Vienna.
2 They said that the police kept the man for a few hours and then released him.
3 She wanted the police to believe that her husband had murdered her.
4 He didn't recognise her at first, because she was wearing a veil.
5 They released him because he had already had his punishment for the murder of his wife.

5 Individual answers required.

# KEY TO PRACTICE SECTION

Unit 5

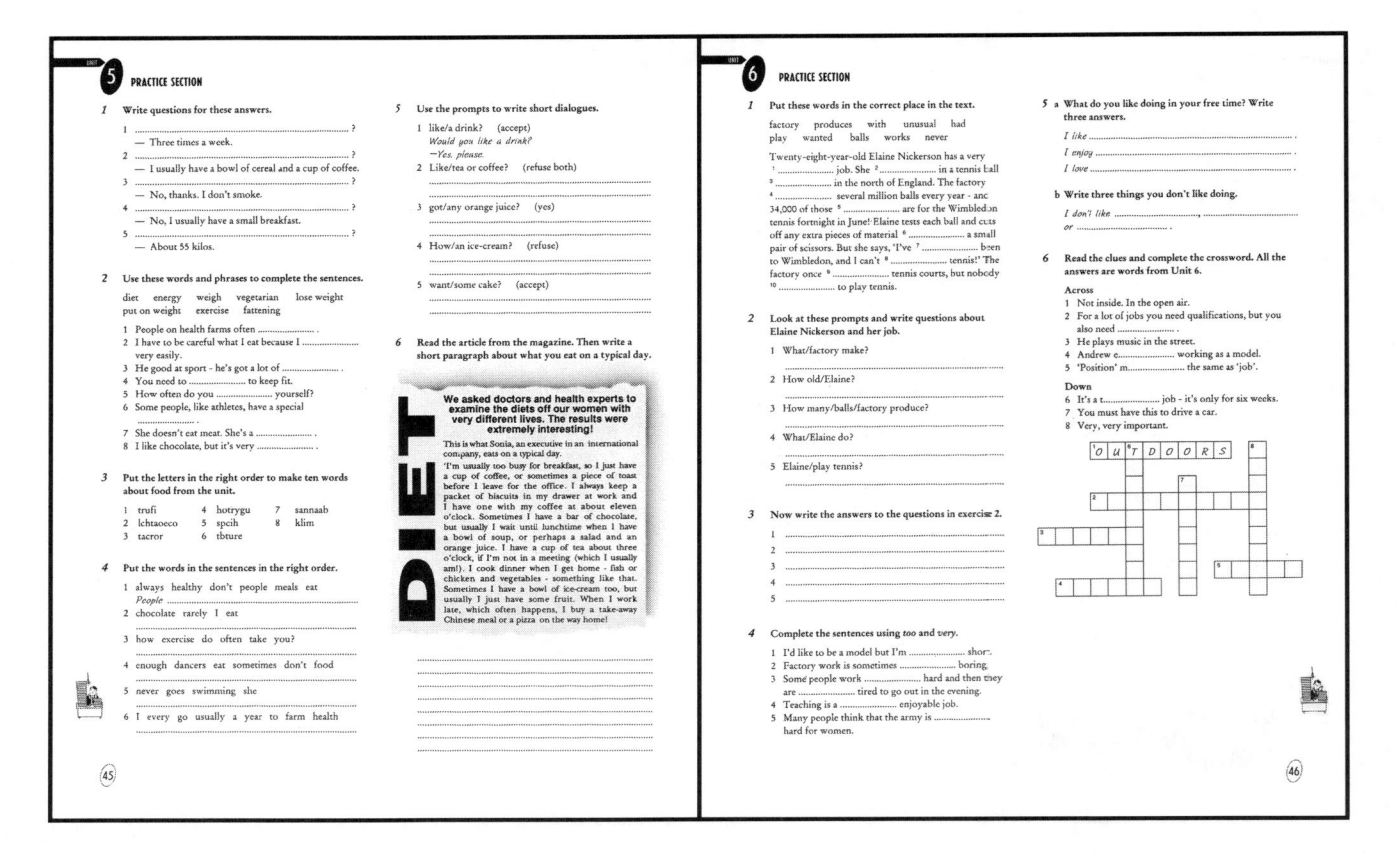

1
1. How often do you play tennis?
2. What do you have for breakfast?
3. Would you like a cigarette?
4. Do you eat a lot for breakfast?
5. How much do you weigh?

2 1 lose weight 2 put on weight 3 energy 4 exercise 5 weigh 6 diet 7 vegetarian 8 fattening

3 1 fruit 2 chocolate 3 carrot 4 yoghurt 5 chips 6 butter 7 bananas 8 milk

4
1. People don't always eat healthy meals.
2. I rarely eat chocolate.
3. How often do you take exercise?
4. Dancers sometimes don't eat enough food.
5. She never goes swimming.
6. I usually go every year to a health farm.

5
1. Would you like tea or coffee? Neither, thanks.
2. Have you got any orange juice. Yes, would you like some?
3. How about an ice-cream? No, thanks.
4. Do you want some cake? Yes, please.

6 Individual answers required.

Unit 6

1 1 unusual 2 works 3 factory 4 produces 5 balls 6 with 7 never 8 play 9 had 10 wanted

2
1. What does the factory make?
2. How old is Elaine?
3. How many balls does the factory produce?
4. What does Elaine do?
5. Does Elaine play tennis?

3
1. The factory makes tennis balls.
2. She's twenty-eight.
3. It produces several million every year.
4. She tests each ball and cuts off any loose pieces of material.
5. No, she doesn't.

4 1 too 2 very 3 very … too 4 very 5 too

5 a, b Individual answers required.

6 **Across:** 1 outdoors 2 experience 3 busker 4 enjoys 5 means
Down: 6 temporary 7 licence 8 essential

KEY TO PRACTICE SECTION

Unit 7

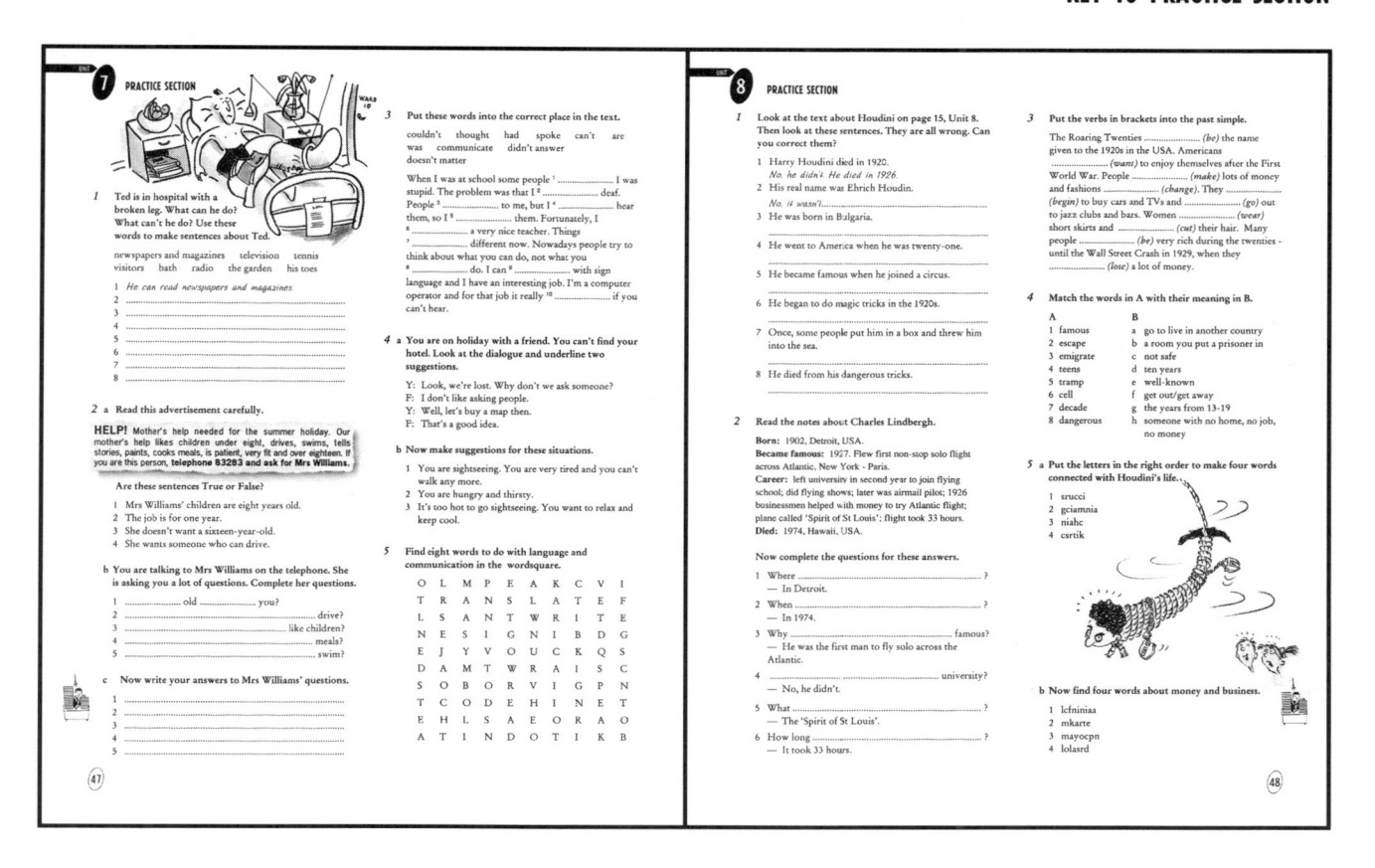

1 2 He can watch television.
   3 He can't play tennis.
   4 He can have visitors.
   5 He can't have a bath.
   6 He can listen to the radio.
   7 He can't work in the garden.
   8 He can't touch his toes.

2 a 1 False 2 False 3 True 4 True

3 b 1 *How* old *are* you? 2 *Can you* drive?
     3 *Do you* like children? 4 *Can you cook* meals?
     5 *Can you* swim?

   c Individual answers required.

3 1 thought 2 was 3 spoke 4 couldn't 5 didn't answer 6 had 7 are 8 can't 9 communicate 10 doesn't matter

4 a *Why don't we* ask someone? 2 Well *let's buy* a map.

   b Individual answers required.

5 **Across:** translate, write, sign, code
  Down: read, speak
  Diagonally: language, say

Unit 8

1 2 No, it wasn't. It was Ehrich Weiss.
   3 No, he wasn't. He was born in Hungary.
   4 No, he didn't. He went when he was a boy.
   5 No, he didn't. He became famous when he began to do escaping tricks.
   6 No, he didn't. He began to do escaping tricks in the 1920s.
   7 No, they didn't. They threw him into a river.
   8 No, he didn't. He died from a stomach disease.

2 1 Where was he born?
   2 When did he die?
   3 Why did he become famous?
   4 Did he finish university?
   5 What was his plane called?
   6 How long did the flight take?

3 was the name *wanted* to enjoy *made* lots of money and fashions *changed* They *began* go out Women *wore* *cut* their hair *were* very rich *lost a* lot of money

4 1e 2f 3a 4g 5h 6b 7d 8c

5 a 1 circus 2 magician 3 chain 4 tricks

   b 1 financial 2 market 3 company 4 dollars

KEY TO PRACTICE SECTION

Unit 9

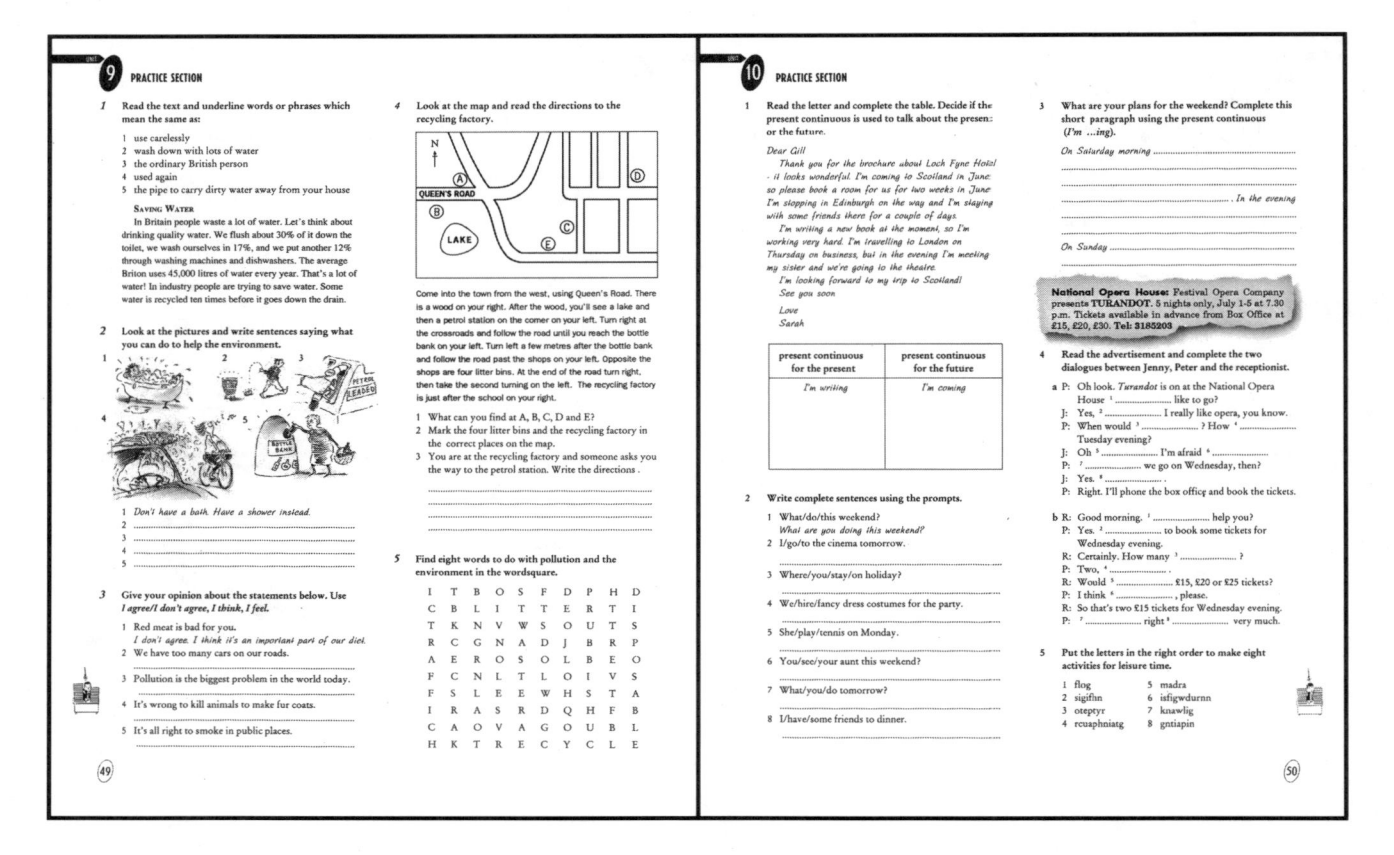

1 1 waste   2 flush   3 the average Briton   4 recycle
5 drain

Suggestions:

2 2 Don't throw litter on the street. Use a litter bin.
3 Don't drive to work. Cycle instead.
4 Don't use leaded petrol. Use unleaded.
5 Don't throw bottles in the bin. Take them to the bottle bank.

3 Individual answers required.

4 1 A: petrol station   B: wood   C: shops   D: school
E: bottle bank
2 Individual answers required.
3 Go straight ahead and at the corner, turn right. Take the first turning on your left and follow the road past the shops to the bottle bank at the corner on your right. Turn right and follow the road past the lake on your left to the crossroads. Cross over the crossroads and the petrol station is on your left.

5 **Across:** litter, aerosol, recycle
Down: traffic, waste, disposable
Diagonally: save, energy

Unit 10

1 **Present continuous for the present:**
1 I'm writing
2 I'm working
3 ... I'm looking forward...
Present continuous for the future:
1 I'm coming to Scotland...   2 I'm stopping in Edinburgh...   3 and I'm staying...   4 I'm travelling..
5 I'm meeting...   6 we're going...

2 2 I'm going to the cinema tomorrow.
3 Where are you staying on holiday?
4 We're hiring fancy dress costumes for the party.
5 She's playing tennis on Monday.
6 Are you seeing your aunt this weekend?
7 What are you doing tomorrow?
8 I'm having some friends to dinner.

3 Individual answers required.

4 a 1 Would   2 I would   3 you like to go?   4 about
5 I can't   6 I'm busy   7 Shall   8 that's great

b 1 can   2 I'd like   3 would you like   4 please
5 you like   6 £15 ones   7 that's   8 thanks

5 1 golf   2 fishing   3 pottery   4 parachuting
5 drama   6 windsurfing   7 walking   8 painting

Unit 11

1 1 decided 2 project 3 asked 4 own 5 refused
6 give up 7 persuaded 8 lend 9 rented 10 bought
11 plans 12 borrow

2 1 How many... 2 How much money... 3 How many...
4 How many... 5 How much ... 6 How many...

3 1 She has one partner.
2 They needed £20,000.
3 They asked ten banks.
4 Two companies lent them money.
5 They needed to borrow £9,000.
6 They have plenty of orders.

4 1d 2h 3j 4i 5b 6a 7e 8c 9f 10g

5 *Suggestions:*
2 Oh, dear. I'm sorry to hear that.
3 That's a pity. Never mind. I'm sure you'll get the next job.
4 How wonderful. You are lucky!
5 What a pity. I hope you can come to the next one.
6 That's fantastic! Congratulations!
7 Oh, well done!
8 I'm sorry to hear that. That's terrible.

Unit 12

1 1 She's 42.
2 She had very romantic ideas about marriage. She thought she and her husband would live happily ever after.
3 He thought she had an easy life, because she didn't have to go out to work.
4 She works part time and she goes out more.
5 They're going to have a party.
6 Her children are going to organise it.

2 2 Where are you going to live?
3 Who is going to look after the children?
4 Are you going to get married this year?
5 When are they going to have the party?
6 Who is going to come to the wedding?

3, 4 Individual answers required.

5 1 waste 2 so 3 agree 4 special 5 married
6 right 7 disagree 8 remember

KEY TO PRACTICE SECTION

Unit 13

Suggestions:

1   2 You must have your passport.
     3 You should buy a guide book at the bookshop.
     4 You should bring some light clothes with you.
     5 You must get a visa from the Chinese Embassy.
     6 You should bring a camera.

2   2f 3a 4g 5e 6b 7d

3 a   1 country   2 speak   3 currency   4 city
       5 usually   6 mild   7 looks   8 weather   9 should
       10 trip

   b   Individual answers required.

Suggestions:

4   1 It's a mountaineering expedition.
     2 The best way is to wear several layers of clothing.
     3 You should wear proper walking boots.
     4 It might be very cold and wet.
     5 You must eat well to keep warm.
     6 You are carrying everything with you, because it's a long expedition and there are no shops or hotels on the way.

5   2 coins   3 travel   4 seatbelt   5 bill   6 weather

Unit 14

1   1 have you been...?   2 Have you always been...?
     3 have always wanted...   4 Have you made...?
     5 have already earned...

2   1 He has studied mathematics ...   2 She wrote her first novel ...   3 I became famous ...   4 ... I have never scored ...   5 Evelyn has been to many ...

3 a   1 She's a TV reporter.
       2 She's 33.
       3 She's single.
       4 She's been to 43 different countries.
       5 She studied French.
       6 She has worked in local radio and TV.

   b   She has reported news from every content and she has been to 43 different countries. She is 33, with red hair and green eyes. She studied French at university and then worked in local radio and TV. She has worked in national TV for five years now.

4   1 Where have you just been?
     2 How long did the trip take?
     3 Had you done this kind of trip before?
     4 I don't believe you!
     5 Have you written a book about it?

5   **Across:** 1 talent   2 heroine   3 autobiography   4 recluse
     Down: 5 champion   6 movie   7 lip   8 genius   9 astonished

KEY TO PRACTICE SECTION

Unit 15

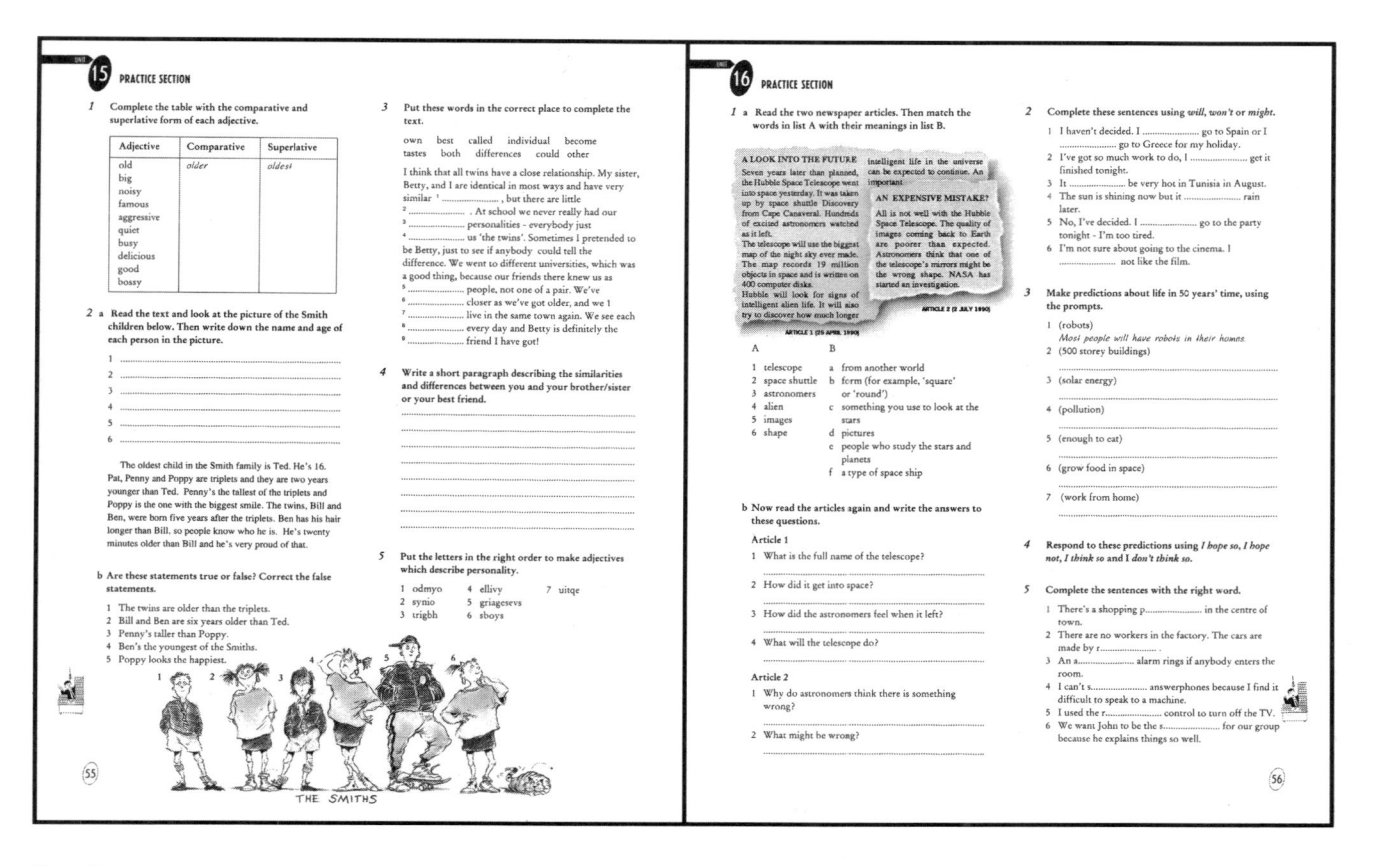

1 Comparatives: bigger, noisier, more famous, more agressive, quieter, busier, more delicious, better, bossier

Superlatives: biggest, noisiest, most famous, most agressive, quietest, busiest, most delicious, best, bossiest

2 a 1 Penny - 14   2 Bill - 9   3 Ted - 16   4 Paula - 14
5 Poppy - 14   6 Ben - 9

b 1 False. The triplets are older than the twins.
2 False. They are seven years younger than Ted.
3 True.
4 False. Bill is the youngest.
5 False. Paula looks the happiest.

3 1 tastes   2 differences   3 own   4 called
5 individual   6 become   7 both   8 other   9 best

4 Individual answers required.

5 1 moody   2 noisy   3 bright   4 lively   5 aggressive
6 bossy   7 quiet

Unit 16

1 a 1c 2f 3e 4a 5d 6b

b 1 The Hubble Space Telescope.
2 It was taken up by the space shuttle Discovery.
3 They felt very excited.
4 It will look for signs of intelligent alien life.

c 1 The quality of images coming back to earth is poorer than expected.
2 One of the telescope's mirrors might be the wrong shape.

2 1 might ... might   2 won't   3 will   4 might   5 won't
6 might

Suggestions:

3 2 Most people will live and work in 500 storey buildings.
3 Most people will use solar energy to heat their homes.
4 There will be no more pollution in the atmosphere.
5 Everybody will have enough to eat.
6 People will be able to grow food in space.
7 Everybody will work from home with a computer.

Suggestions:

4 1 I hope so.   2 I don't think so.   3 I think so.
4 I hope so.   5 I hope so.   6 I don't think so.
7 I hope not.

5 1 precinct   2 robots   3 automatic   4 stand
5 remote   6 spokesperson

KEY TO PRACTICE SECTION

Unit 17

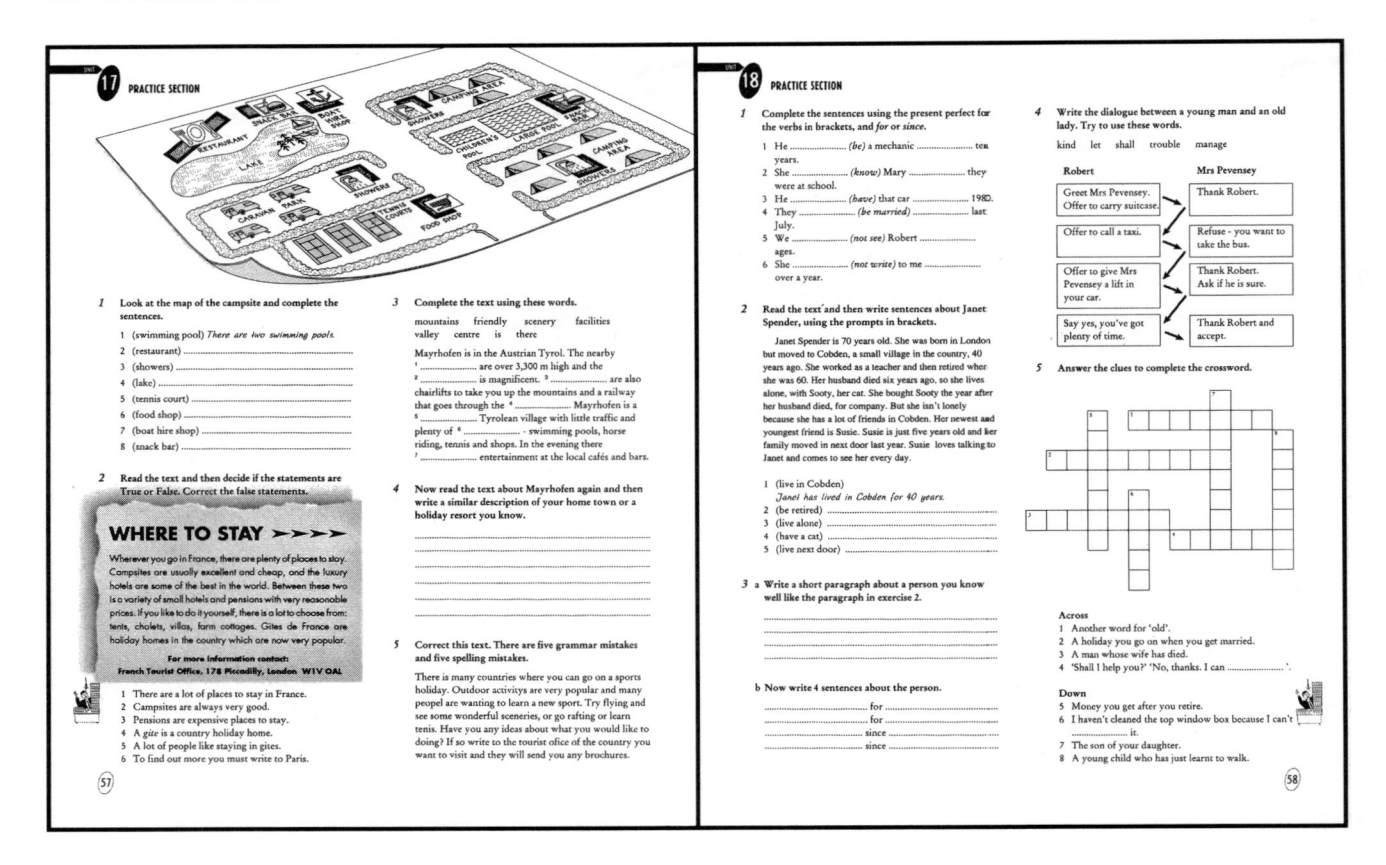

1 2 There is one restaurant. 3 There are three showers. 4 There is one lake. 5 There are three tennis courts. 6 There is one food shop. 7 There is one boat hire shop. 8 There are two snack bars.

2 1 True.
2 False. They are *usually* very good.
3 False. They are not expensive.
4 True.
5 True.
7 False. You can write to the French Tourist Office in London.

3 1 mountains 2 scenery 3 there 4 valley 5 friendly 6 facilities 7 is

4 Individual answers required.

5 Spelling mistakes: *peopel* - people; *tenis* - tennis; *ofice* - office; *broshures* - brochures; *activitys* - activities

Grammar mistakes: *is* - are; *are wanting* - want; *sceneries* - scenery; *to doing* - to do; *any* - some

Unit 18

1 1 He has been a mechanic for 10 years.
2 She has known Mary since they were at school.
3 He has had that car since 1980.
4 They have been married since last July.
5 We have not seen Robert for ages.
6 She has not written to me for over a year.

2 2 She has been retired for 10 years.
3 She has lived alone for six years.
4 She has had a cat since her husband died.
5 Susie has lived next door since last year.

3 a,b Individual answers required.

Suggestion:
4 Robert: Hello, Mrs Pevensey. Let me take your suitcase.
Mrs P: Thanks a lot. It's quite heavy.
Robert: Shall I call a taxi?
Mrs P: Oh, no thanks. I can manage. I want to take the bus.
Robert: Would you like a lift in my car?
Mrs P: Thank you. Are you sure it's no trouble?
Robert: No, I've got plenty of time.
Mrs P: Thanks very much. That's very kind.

5 Across: 1 elderly 2 honeymoon 3 widower 4 manage
Down: 5 pension 6 reach 7 grandson 8 toddler

… KEY TO PRACTICE SECTION

Unit 19

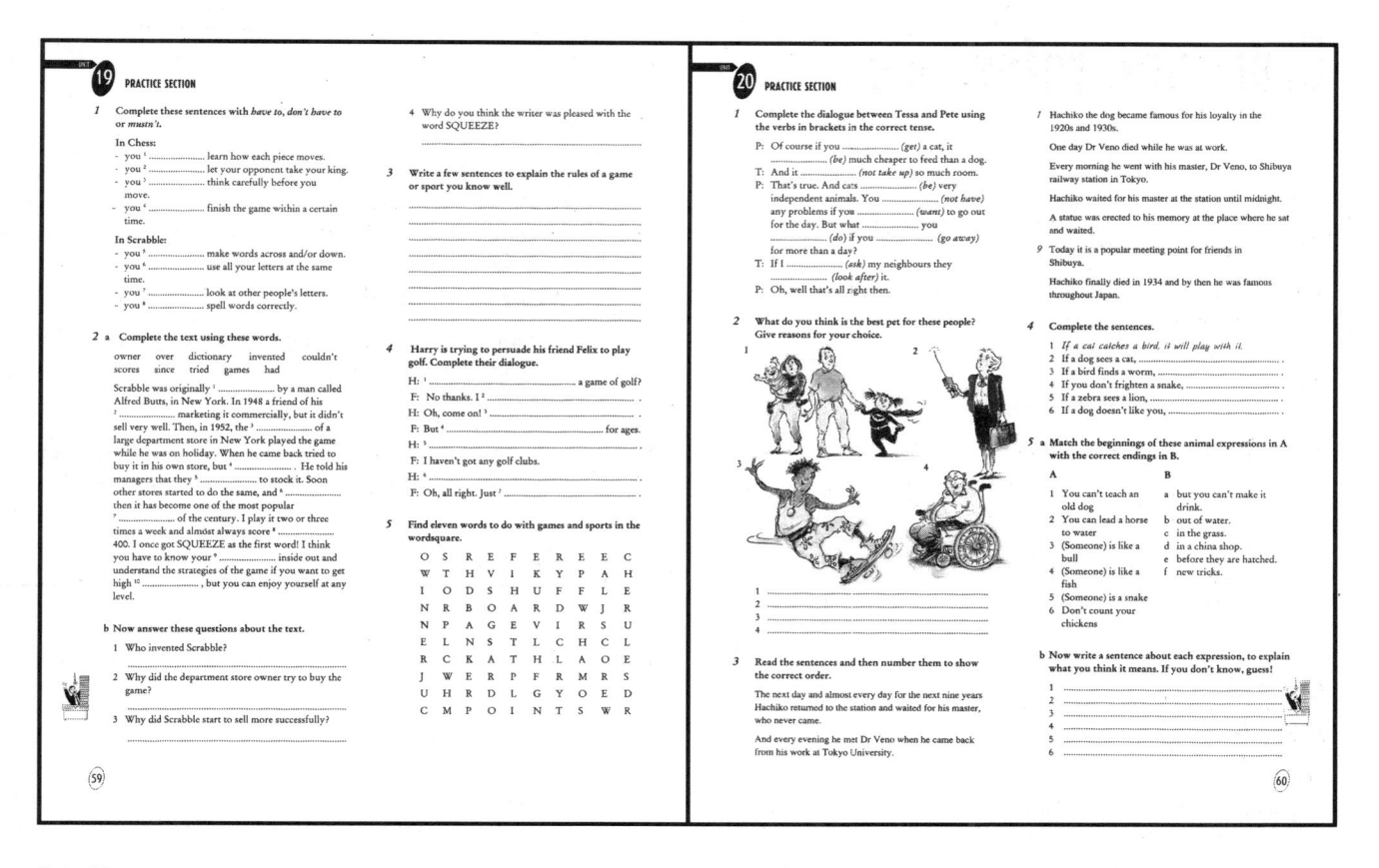

1 1 have to   2 mustn't   3 have to   4 don't have to
   5 have to   6 don't have to   7 mustn't   8 have to

2 a 1 invented   2 tried   3 owner   4 couldn't   5 had
      6 since   7 games   8 over   9 dictionary   10 scores

   b 1 Alfred Butts invented it.
      2 He tried to buy it because he wanted to play it at home.
      3 It started to sell more because other stores began to stock it.
      4 He was pleased with it because he used the letters q, u and z and they carry very high scores.

3 Individual answers required.

Suggestion:

4 1 How about...   2 I don't like golf.   3 You'll enjoy it!
   4 ...I haven't played for ages.   5 That's o.k. Neither have I.   6 I'll lend you some golf clubs.   7 ...one game.

5 **Across:** referee, shuffle, board, points
   Down: winner, banker, score, rules
   Diagonally: card, throw, cheat

Unit 20

1 P: ... get a cat ... it will be much cheaper...
   T: ... will not take up.
   P: ... are... won't ... want ... do ... do ... go away
   T: ... ask ... will look after

2 Individual answers required.

3 Every morning he went with his master, Dr Veno, to Shibuya railway station in Tokyo. And every evening he met Dr Veno when he came back from his work at Tokyo University. One day Dr Veno died while he was at work. Hachiko waited for his master at the station until midnight. The next day and almost every day for the next nine years Hachiko returned to the station and waited for his master, who never came. Hachiko finally died in 1934 and by then he was famous throughout Japan. A statue was erected to his memory at the place where he sat and waited. Today it is a popular meeting point for friends in Shibuya.

4 2 ... it will chase it.
   3 ... it will eat it.
   4 ... it won't bite you.
   5 ... it will run away.
   6 ... it will growl.

5 a 1f 2a 3d 4b 5c 6e

   b Individual answers required.

50

Grammar reference

Unit 1
The present simple

1. You use the present simple most commonly to talk about:
   a) regular or habitual actions.
      I *go* to work every day.
   b) facts
      Toledo *is* a Spanish city.

2. *Yes/no questions: short answers*

   | Is | she/he | happy? | — Yes (No) | she/he is (isn't). |
   | Are | they | | | they are (aren't). |

   | Do | you | live here? | — Yes (No) | I do (don't). |
   | Does | she/he | | | she/he does (doesn't). |

Unit 2
Have/have got

1. *Have got* is often used instead of *have* in spoken British English. In written texts, *have* is more common.
   'I*'ve got* an umbrella.'
   Heathrow *has* four terminals.

2. *Have got* can also be used in questions, and can be answered using a short answer or an extended answer.
   Have you *got* any brothers or sisters?
   — Yes, I *have*. I*'ve got* two sisters.
   Note that in the short answer, *have* is used rather than *have got*.

3. *Have got* is often less formal than *have*.
   Do you have a ticket? Formal
   Have you got any tickets left? Informal

Unit 3
The present continuous

1. The form of the present continuous is:

I	am	
She/He	is	eating.
You/We/They	are	

2. You use the present continuous to talk about:
   a) something that is happening at the moment you are speaking.
      What *are you doing*? — I*'m washing* my hair.
   b) a temporary situation.
      I *am collecting* money for a trip across Africa.
   c) changes and development.
      Their writing *is improving* all the time.

3. You often use a time expression when you want to show that you are talking about the present time.
   She *is writing* a book *at the moment*.

Want to + infinitive

Certain verbs to do with hopes and wishes cannot be used in the present continuous, but take *to* + infinitive clause after the verb.
   She *wants to be* comfortable.
Some other verbs which cannot be used in the present continuous tense include *hope*, *expect* and *wish*.

Unit 4
The past simple

1. The past simple is formed by adding *-ed* to the infinitive root.
   start   start*ed*
   move   mov*ed*
   retire   retir*ed*
   See the irregular verbs table in the Teacher's Book for a list of common irregular verbs. See Unit 8 for the past simple in negatives and questions.

2. You use the past simple if you want to say:
   a) that something happened in the past.
      They *shared* rooms in Baker Street.
   b) that something happened at a particular time in the past.
      He *retired* in 1903.

Unit 5
Adverbs of frequency

1. You use an adverb of frequency to show how many times something happens.
   She *often* goes to the cinema.

2. You can put the adverb in different positions but it is usually:
   a) after the verb *to be*.
      She *is always* happy.
      They *aren't usually* late.
   b) before other verbs.
      He *rarely speaks* in the morning.
      We *never eat* in restaurants.

Unit 6

Like + gerund

You use *like* + gerund if you are talking simply about likes and dislikes.

    She *likes* work*ing* from home.
    He *likes* go*ing* out.

Note that *would you like ...?* is always followed by an infinitive.

    Would you like to come to the party?

Too and *very*

1. You use *too* to give something a negative meaning.
    My feet are *too* big. (I can't find any shoes that fit me.)
    It was *too* hot. (So we couldn't go out.)

2. You use *very* to emphasise something.
    My feet are *very* big. (But I can still find shoes to wear.)
    It was *very* hot. (But not too hot.)

Note that you cannot use *too* instead of *very*.
    * I am *too* happy to meet you.
    I am *very* happy to meet you.

Unit 7

Can for ability

You use *can* to say that someone has a skill or ability, or that they are able to do something. You use it followed by the base form of a verb.

I/You/She/He/We/They	can cannot/can't	swim.

Unit 8

The past simple in negatives and questions

See Unit 4 for uses of the past simple.

1. When making negatives and questions in the past, you use *did*. The main verb is in the infinitive.

Negative

I/You/He/She/We/They	did not/didn't	see him yesterday.

Question

Did	I/you/she/he/they	give him the money?

2. With the verb *to be*, *did* is not used in negatives and questions.

Negative

| I/She/He | was not/wasn't | at home last night. |
| You/We/They | were not/weren't | |

Question

| Was | I/she/he | right? |
| Were | you/we/they | |

Unit 9

The imperative

1. You use the imperative when you want:
   a) to tell someone to do or not to do something.
      Stop him!
      Don't touch that!
   b) to give advice or a warning.
      Be careful.

2. Advice or warnings are often expressed in the negative.
    Don't be afraid of them.
    Don't go there. It's not very good.

3. The negative can also be formed by putting *never* in front of the base form of a verb.
    Never open the door without looking.

Unit 10

The present continuous for future arrangements

See Unit 3 for present continuous form.

You can use the present continuous to talk about a particular time in the future. You can use a time expression to make it clear that you are talking about the future. This is not necessary when the event is understood to be in the future.

    We're having a meeting *on Thursday afternoon*.
    — Who *is coming*?

Unit 11

How much...?/How many...?

You use *How many* with plural countable nouns, and *How much* with uncountable nouns. See Unit 17 for information on (un)countable nouns.

    How many languages can you speak?
    — Not many./Lots.
    How much money did you spend on it?
    — Not much./A lot.

GRAMMAR REFERENCE

Unit 12

Going to + infinitive for future plans

1. You use *going to* + infinitive to for your future plans and intentions.

I	'm/am	
She/He	's/is	going to get married next year.
You/We/They	're/are	

   Questions

What	is	she/he	going to do?
	are	you/we/they	

Is	she/he	going to visit her?
	you/we/they	

2. You can use the present continuous instead of *going to* + infinitive, but this means that arrangements have been made.

   My brother's getting married next Saturday. (date given)
   I'm not going to get married. (no special plans made yet)

Unit 13

Must, should and *can*

1. You use *must/must not* to say that:
   a) something is required by a rule or a law.
      You *must* put your seatbelt on for take-off and landing.
      You *mustn't* smoke during take-off.
   b) something has to be done because you feel it is important.
      You *must* come at once. Your house is on fire.

2. You use *should/should not*:
   a) when you are advising someone to do/not to do something.
      You *should* wash your hands before you eat.
      You really *shouldn't* go out alone at night.
   b) when you are saying that something is the right thing to do.
      We *should* send her a postcard.

3. You use *can/cannot* to say that someone is allowed to/not allowed to do something.
   You *can* go now.
   You *cannot* go in there. It's private.
   Note that this is not the same as *can* for ability. See Unit 7.

Unit 14

The present perfect

1. The form of the present perfect is:

I/You/We/They	have	
She/He	has	visited many countries.

   Questions

Have	you/we/they	
Has	she/he	finished?

2. You use the present perfect for something that happened in the past but not at a specific time.
   He *has been* to England.

   It also connects a past action or event to the present.
   I *have lived* in England all my life.

Unit 15

Comparative and superlative adjectives

1. Comparative adjectives consist of the adjective + *-er* for one or two syllable adjectives. When the adjective ends in a *y* this is changed to an *i*.
   My brother is *younger* than me.
   She is much *happier* than she was yesterday.
   When the adjective is longer than two syllables, *more* is placed in front of it.
   This book is *more interesting* than the last one I read.

2. Superlative adjectives consist of *the* + adjective + *-est* for one or two syllable adjectives. When the adjective ends in a *y* this is changed to an *i*.
   He is *the richest* man in the country.
   July is *the busiest* month at this hotel.
   When the adjective is longer than two syllables, *most* is placed in front of it.
   They are *the most famous* twins in history.

3. Irregular forms of comparative and superlative adjectives are:
   good   better   best
   bad   worse   worst

Unit 16

Future certainty and possibility

1. You use *will* and *won't* to talk about future certainty.
   People *will have* more free time.
   People *won't work* after the age of 50.

2. You use *might/might not* to talk about future possibility.
   People *might visit* Mars.
   He *might not arrive* on time.

Unit 17

Countable and uncountable nouns

1. You use countable nouns to refer to people or things that you can count. They have a plural form.
    The mountains look beautiful.
    The beaches are very clean.
   They are usually preceded by a number or determiner (*a* or *the*).

2. You use uncountable nouns to refer to general things rather than objects. You cannot count them, and they do not have a plural form.
    There was *food* for everybody in the hall.
    The *scenery* was magnificent.

   You do not use these nouns with numbers, but you can use expressions such as *some/a lot of*.
    I need *some* paper.
    There was *a lot of* rain.

There is/there are

You use *there is* and *there are* to talk about something that exists.
 There is some magnificent scenery.
 There are seven Land Rovers.

Unit 18

The present perfect continuous

1. You use the present perfect continuous to describe activities that started in the past, continued and are still happening now.

   | I/You/We/They | have/'ve | been saving up to go on |
   | She/He | has/'s | holiday. |

2. If you want to describe the duration of the event you use:
   a) *for* to emphasise how long something lasts.
        We *have been waiting for* an hour.
   b) *since* to show when something started.
        He's *been working* in London *since* January.

Unit 19

Have to + infinitive

1. *Have* + *to* and *must* have similar meanings. *Must* means there is a rule and *have to* usually means a rule you have made yourself.
    You *must* put out your cigarettes.
    = There is a rule which tells you to do this.
    I *have to* stop smoking.
    = I have decided to stop smoking.
   Note that in the negative, their meanings are different.
    You *must not* leave the room.
    = You are not allowed to leave the room.
    You *don't have to* leave the room.
    = You can leave the room if you want to, but it is not necessary.

2. You can use *have to* to say that something is necessary or extremely important.
    You *have to listen* carefully to understand what he says.

3. You can use *have to* without an infinitive if the infinitive is understood.
    Why do you get up so early?
    — I *have to*. I start work at eight.

Unit 20

When and *if* in the first conditional

1. You use the first conditional to describe something that is going to happen. There are two parts to the sentence. The first part describes the event and the second part describes the results of the event. In the first part of the sentence, *when* and *if* are followed by the present tense.

   | When you go to the shop | you won't know what to choose. |
   | If he comes soon | we will catch the train. |

2. You can reverse the order of the two parts of the sentence.
    If it's fine tomorrow, we'*ll* go for a walk.
    We'*ll* go for a walk *if* it's fine tomorrow.

3. You use *when* to show that you expect something to happen and *if* to show that something might/might not happen.
    When I see her, I'*ll* tell her. (I know I will see her.)
    If I see her, I'*ll* tell her. (I'm not sure that I will see her.)

Tapescripts

I = Interviewer   M = Man   W = Woman   B = Boy

Unit 1

Exercise 2: Personal information

Part 1

- **W** So, let's get a form and I can fill in a few personal details.
- **J** Mhmm.
- **W** Here we are. Now, first name, Jo-sette.
- **J** That's right.
- **W** I've got your address here. Just a moment. Now, what's your surname, Josette?
- **J** Aparis.
- **W** A-P-A-R-E ...?
- **J** No, I. A-P-A-R-I-S.
- **W** Right. And female. Now, what about your friend? Are you looking for a male or female friend, or either?
- **J** Male. I have quite a lot of female friends, but I don't know many men here.
- **W** OK. So your ideal friend is male. And you're French?
- **J** That's right.
- **W** Now, what about your friend's nationality?
- **J** Oh, it doesn't matter. Er, well, I don't want French because I'm learning English here, so someone who speaks English.
- **W** OK. So, any nationality but a native English speaker or a good English speaker.
- **J** Yes.
- **W** Right. What do you do, Josette?
- **J** I'm a student.
- **W** Student. And how old are you?
- **J** 21.
- **W** And your friend? Do you want someone the same age as you?
- **J** Yes. Well, er, in his twenties.
- **W** So, between twenty and thirty.
- **J** Yes.
- **W** Right. And how tall are you Josette ...?

Part 2

- **W** Now, here you put your interests. For example, are you interested in travel, any particular sport ...
- **J** Right. Er, that's OK. I'm interested in travel, not, er, in the theatre. So I put a tick here beside travel. Er, and what about this question here - music?
- **W** Yes, what kind of music do you like? Do you like classical music, pop music ...
- **J** Well, er, I like all kinds of music really.
- **W** So, tick music and write 'all kinds of music' in the space.
- **J** And here I describe myself?
- **W** Yes, for example, are you shy or sociable, friendly, serious ...
- **J** Oh dear. Er, I'm not sure. I'm quite serious, I suppose, but, er, not very shy.
- **W** When you've finished, answer the question at the bottom. Do you smoke?
- **J** Yes, I do.
- **W** And what about your friend? Do you want someone who smokes or a non-smoker?
- **J** Oh, it doesn't matter.
- **W** OK. Just write 'not important' here. Then you sign at the bottom here ...

Exercise 6: Small talk

Dialogue A

- **M1** Hi!
- **M2** Hi. OK?
- **M1** Yeah. Fine. You?
- **M2** Not bad, thanks. See you.
- **M1** Yeah. Cheerio.

Dialogue B

- **M** Well, thanks very much. That was very helpful. And it was very nice meeting you Mrs Cunningham.
- **W** And you. And I look forward to our meeting next month in New York. Goodbye, Mr Stevens.
- **M** Goodbye.

Dialogue C

- **B1** Dad, this is Michael. Michael, my father.
- **B2** How do you do, Mr Barnes?
- **M** I'm very pleased to meet you, Michael.
- **B1** And this is my sister, Theresa.
- **B2** Pleased to meet you, Theresa.
- **W** Hello.
- **M** Well, sit down, Michael. Here, let me take your coat.

Dialogue D

- **M1** Good morning, Janet.
- **W** Good morning. Cold today, isn't it?
- **M2** Yes, freezing. Good morning, Bob.
- **M1** Morning. How are you?
- **M2** Fine, thanks.
- **M1** Good. Janet. Have you got those letters ...?

Dialogue E

- **W1** Goodnight.
- **W2** Goodnight, Yvonne. Thanks for a lovely meal.
- **M** Yes, it was really nice. Thanks a lot.
- **W1** Glad you enjoyed it. See you on Friday.
- **M** Yes. OK. Goodnight.
- **W2** Bye.
- **W1** Night.

Unit 2

Exercise 2: A home of my own

Dialogue A

- **I** Who do you live with, Willem?
- **W** With two friends.
- **I** And do you live in Amsterdam, or near Amsterdam?
- **W** We live in an old windmill about twenty kilometres from Amsterdam.
- **I** A windmill! Really?
- **W** Yes, the three of us bought it two years ago and we all worked together to put in a kitchen and a bathroom and so on.
- **I** You did the work yourselves?
- **W** Yes, most of it. Someone helped us build new floors and ceilings, but we did about 80% of the work ourselves.
- **I** That's really good.
- **W** Yes. We love it. And it's very comfortable now with a proper kitchen, living room and everyone has got their own bedroom. But we haven't got any electricity or central heating yet.

Dialogue B

- **I** Hiro, you live in Japan, don't you?
- **H** That's right. I've got my own flat near the centre.
- **I** What's your flat like? Is it a modern one?
- **H** Yes. It's in a modern block. It's small - most flats in Tokyo are very small. Mine has got one room and a very small kitchen. It's tiny really, and it hasn't got a bathroom, just a toilet.
- **I** So where do you have a bath?
- **H** In the public baths on my street. A lot of people in Tokyo use the public baths.
- **I** And the living room and bedroom are the same room?
- **H** That's right. And outside the living room there's a balcony. I grow lots of plants on the balcony. It's small, but I like it a lot.

Dialogue C

- **I** Whereabouts in France do you live, Florence?
- **F** In the north, in a small village called Duclair.
- **I** Do you live by yourself?
- **F** No, with my family - even my grandparents live with us!
- **I** So what's your house like? I suppose it's quite big if all the family live there.
- **F** Yes, it's very big.
- **I** How many bedrooms has it got?
- **F** Seven, but we need them all because I've got two brothers and two sisters. Then there's me, my parents and grandparents. My grandparents have their own kitchen and bathroom.
- **I** So it's got two kitchens and two bathrooms?
- **F** No - three bathrooms! One for my grandparents, one for my parents and one for the children. Yes, it is a huge old house and it's got a beautiful garden at the back. I love it.
- **I** And you've got your own bedroom?
- **F** Yes, it's in the attic at the top of the house.

Exercise 5: Designs on a room

- **ID** Now, I designed this bedroom last year. It's quite similar in shape and size to yours.
- **M** Mhmm. It looks bigger than mine. It's very nice.
- **ID** Yes. The colours and the space in the middle make it look bigger. But it was about five metres by five.
- **M** What's that? About fifteen feet by fifteen?
- **ID** Yes. You see it's a square room, like yours. And I put the table here, under the window for maximum light.
- **M** Mhmm.
- **ID** And the bed against this wall, opposite the door. You see, this wall had no doors or radiators or anything so we had the length of the wall for the bed and at each side the two fitted wardrobes.
- **M** Yes. They look very nice, and I need a lot of storage space.
- **ID** That's right. These wardrobes have got a lot space inside.
- **M** Mhmm. And what about drawers? There isn't a chest of drawers in the room.
- **ID** No. The wardrobes have got a set of drawers inside. You see, if we put nearly all the furniture along this wall there is much more space in the room. And, as you can see, the whole room is decorated in very pale colours which make it look bigger. And for a splash of colour, I put this very colourful Chinese rug in the middle of the room.
- **M** Yes. It looks lovely.
- **ID** Now, this one is quite different. It's much more colourful and ...

Unit 3

Exercise 4: Dreams come true

- **DJ** So let's hear some ambitions for the New Year and tell us what you're doing to realise these ambitions. Ambitions big or small, let's hear from you. OK, Sue. Go ahead.
- **S** Hello.
- **DJ** Hello, Sue. So what's your ambition for this year?
- **S** To go to Hong Kong.
- **DJ** How old are you, Sue?
- **S** 18.
- **DJ** And why Hong Kong? Have you got friends there?
- **S** No. I've seen lots of pictures of Hong Kong and it looks fantastic. I just want to go.
- **DJ** That's quite an expensive trip.
- **S** I know. So, I'm working in a factory at the moment to save the money. I'm packing boxes nine hours a day, six days a week.
- **DJ** And are you enjoying it?
- **S** No, definitely not. But I'm saving money and next month I'll have enough money to buy the ticket - I hope.
- **DJ** Well, all the best, Sue, and I hope you have a great time in Hong Kong. And next on the line is Alan. Hello, Alan.
- **A** Hello, Dave. You want to know my ambition?
- **DJ** We certainly do.
- **A** I'm running twenty miles every day at the moment

TAPESCRIPTS

because I want to enter for the New York Marathon next year.

DJ I admire you, Alan. Do you think you've got the right experience?

A Oh, yes. I ran in the London Marathon last year and I did quite well, so I want to make the New York one this year.

DJ And how's the training going?

A Fine, but I'm losing a lot of weight right now so I'm watching my diet very carefully.

DJ Well, all the best, Alan. And don't overdo it. Now we've got Matthew ready to talk to us. Matthew, can you tell us your ambition for this year?

M Hello. Yes, well, this is something I've wanted to do for a long time. I want to pass my driving test before my fortieth birthday.

DJ Do you need to learn to drive for your job?

M Oh, no. I just want to do it for myself.

DJ Well, when is your fortieth birthday?

M In two years time.

DJ Two years? You've got plenty of time.

M Well, not really. You see I've been trying for fifteen years now and I've failed seventeen times.

DJ Oh dear.

M I know. It's terrible. I'm having lessons every day now. I've got my test next month and I'm already feeling nervous.

DJ Well, the best of luck, Matthew. I'll keep my fingers crossed ...

Exercise 6: A driving ambition

R Good morning, Peak Driving School.

S Oh, good morning. I'm phoning about driving lessons.

R Yes ...

S The thing is my father's teaching me, but I want to have some lessons from a school as well. Is that possible?

R Certainly. You have a test lesson with us so we can see how you drive, and then we tell you how many more lessons you need.

S I see ... and how much does each lesson cost?

R Fifteen pounds fifty for one hour.

S Right, could I book the test lesson then, please?

R Yes of course. Er, how about next Wednesday at four o'clock?

S Wednesday at four ... yes, that's fine.

R And could I have your name and address, please?

S Sarah Jones, 12 Station Road.

R Thank you Miss Jones. Goodbye.

S Thanks, goodbye.

Unit 4

Exercise 2: Elementary, my dear Watson!

I My guest today, Alison Thomas, has just written a book about one of the greatest detectives of all time, Sherlock Holmes. Alison, can you tell us a bit about your book?

A Certainly. It's about his life. I'm most interested in what happened to him after he gave up his detective work. We know a lot about Sherlock Holmes, the detective, but we don't really know what happened to him after that. He retired at quite an early age, you know. He was only about fifty.

I So what did he do after he retired?

A Well, that's the interesting thing, nobody really knows.

I Perhaps he got tired and wanted to lead a quiet life?

A Maybe, but I don't think so. Some people think that he became a spy. I think he continued to work because he was such an active and energetic person - not really the kind of person to retire early. He probably worked for the government in some way. He knew a lot of famous people and he had an active mind. Other people think he retired just to study bees, but I'm not so sure.

I Perhaps he got married.

A Oh, no. I'm sure he didn't. He wasn't interested in marriage. No, I don't think he got married and I don't think he retired.

I So what about his earlier life ...

Exercise 4: The Woman in Black

The man and the woman were husband and wife. Twenty years ago the woman had run away with another man. She wanted everyone to believe she was dead. So before she disappeared, she sent a note to the police to say she thought her husband wanted to kill her and that she was very scared. The next day she shot off two of her fingers and left them in the garden. The police came to the house, found the woman had disappeared and found her fingers in the garden. They arrested the husband for murder and he spent the next twenty years in prison. The day the man got on the train to Vienna was the day of his release from prison. He had only his old clothes which he wore the day he was arrested. That's why they looked very old-fashioned. When he got on the train, he thought he recognised the woman but he couldn't see her face because of the veil. As soon as she took off her gloves, he was sure it was his wife. He jumped up, told the woman who he was and strangled her. People in the train heard the noise and came rushing to the compartment but too late, he had murdered his wife. The police arrested him, but when they found it was the man who had just been in prison for the last twenty years for his wife's murder, they released him because he had already had his punishment.

Unit 5

Exercise 5: A dancer's diet

I Gill, as a professional dancer, are you very careful about what you eat?

G Not at all. I eat what I want, really. Although I never have lunch because I'm always too busy practising. I just drink lots of water during the day. But I usually have quite a big breakfast.

I What do you have?

G Oh, cereal with milk or yoghurt, toast, maybe one or

two pieces, with jam, cheese or sometimes a boiled egg. I never eat butter, though, only margarine.
I And for dinner?
G A normal meal. Er - fish, chips, vegetables or chicken, rice er, pasta and sauce. Something like that. Not much red meat, more fish or chicken. I suppose I eat lots of fruit and raw vegetables, like salad and grated carrots. I know some dancers who never eat anything fattening. I have a friend, for example. She nearly kills herself trying to stay thin. I don't agree with that.
I What kind of things does she eat, then?
G Oh, er lemon tea for breakfast. She never eats anything in the morning. Then maybe a carrot at lunchtime and she usually has a bit of plain yoghurt and lemon juice for dinner. On Sunday she sometimes has a piece of grilled chicken and salad. But that's all.
I Goodness. That's not very much!
G No. I was like that myself a few years ago. I watched every little thing I ate and I only weighed about 40 kilos, but I often felt sick at the end of the day. I'm fine now. I'm never sick.

Exercise 6: Offering food and drink

Dialogue A

W How about a drink?
M Yes, please. I'll have a beer.
W They don't sell beer here! It's all mineral water and carrot juice!
M Oh, sorry, I forgot. I'll have an orange juice then, please.
W Ice?
M Yes, please.
W Anything to eat?
M No, not just now thanks.

Dialogue B

Wa Would you like tea or coffee, madam?
W I'll have coffee, please.
Wa Sir?
M Er, tea for me please ... thanks.
Wa Cream or milk, madam?
W Neither, thank you.
Wa Sir?
M Have you got any lemon?
Wa Certainly, sir. Here you are.
M That's great. Thank you.

Unit 6

Exercise 4: Position vacant

M In this advert here it says 'Experienced cook wanted'. What does 'experienced' mean?
W It means, er, they've done this job before. This is not their first job as a cook so they know a lot about cooking.
M Right. I see. And what about this word? In this advert about tour guides. It says 'No qualifications necessary'. Can you explain the meaning of 'qualifications'?

W Er, it's the same as exams or diplomas. So 'no qualifications' means you don't need to have passed any exams to do this job.
M OK. Thanks. I understand it now.
W Anything else?
M No, thanks. Everything else is fine.

Exercise 6: Unusual jobs

Dialogue A

I Andrew, your job is quite unusual for a man, isn't it?
A Not really. There are a lot of male models. But I suppose being a model is more popular with women than men.
I And you enjoy your job?
A I love it. I'm lucky to earn money from something I really enjoy. And I enjoy training too.
I Training?
A Well, yes. We have to keep fit, eat well, you know to keep looking good. But I like weight training and I love swimming and walking, so it's no problem for me.
I And do you earn a lot?
A I can earn £500 a day, but there are some days, of course, when I don't have any work. That's what I don't like. I hate waiting for the phone to ring, waiting for that next job. But I like working hard for a few days and then having a few days off. But one problem is you sometimes have to do quite dangerous jobs.
I Dangerous?
A Yes. One time I nearly killed myself when I had to do a job skiing down a mountain. There was an avalanche and I'm not even a good skier. I was scared I can tell you. So I don't like doing dangerous jobs but most jobs are OK. No, usually it's good fun and I love travelling and I've been to some interesting places.

Dialogue B

I Jason, you have a very unusual job. Can you tell me something about it?
J Yes, well, I'm a busker, or street entertainer. So I bring my music here to the Square and dance. I love dancing so it's a great job for me. But I don't like coming out in the bad weather, you know, if it's too cold or too wet. So I do most of my work in spring and summer. Lots of people come in the summer, and if they like my dancing they put money in the hat. My partner takes the hat round during the show. Some people give a lot, some just a few pence.
I Do you get a lot of money?
J Some days I do. In the summer, I can get over a hundred a day.
I A hundred pounds a day?
J Yes, maybe more. But next year I'm going to try in Paris. It's too difficult here with the police, sometimes. Like - I don't like thinking about the police all the time - you know, are they going to tell me I'm making too much noise, that kind of thing. People tell me it's much better in Paris.
I Well, all the best. I think you're a great dancer.
J Thanks.

TAPESCRIPTS

Unit 7
Exercise 5: Can you read Japanese?
- **I** Hiro, can you tell us something about the Japanese language? It looks so difficult to read and write.
- **H** Yes. It's not really difficult.
- **I** But there are so many characters or symbols. How can you learn them all?
- **H** Well, there are a lot of characters in the Japanese language. Maybe about five or six thousand but nobody knows all of them.
- **I** How many do you know?
- **H** About two thousand. But I was a university student, so I can do more than some people. For example, when you leave secondary school you should know about eight hundred then you can read most things.
- **I** So children learn them slowly at school?
- **H** That's right. They just learn a few every week.
- **I** But how can young children read books if they only know a few characters? You mean they can only begin to read books when they are about fourteen years old?
- **H** No. There are lots of books for children but we have another alphabet, a very simple one, that children learn first.
- **I** Another alphabet?
- **H** Yes. It's called Hiragana.
- **I** How does it work?
- **H** Well, for example, I come from Yokohama in Japan so my town has four sounds: yo-ko-ha-ma. And there is one Japanese letter for yo, one for ko, one for ha and one for ma, so yo-ko-ha-ma has four letters. There are about 46 basic letters and each one is a Japanese sound.
- **I** So that's called Hir-, er Hira?
- **H** Hiragana.
- **I** What do you call the other system - the difficult one?
- **H** It's called Kanji.
- **I** And Kanji is from Chinese, isn't it?
- **H** That's right. Yes. About two thousand years ago, people couldn't write Japanese and then they learned the Chinese writing system and used the Chinese characters to write Japanese words. So we write the same as the Chinese but we say it differently.

Exercise 6: Code cracking
- **M** What's this? 'Cracking the Code'. What do we do?
- **W** Well, these numbers are instead of letters. We find which number is which letter.
- **M** So, maybe 1 is A and 2 is B and so on.
- **W** Let's try that. Mhmm. No. That can't be right. Look, 2426, B - a, b, c, d, D. BDB, - a, b, c, d, e, f, F. BDBF? That's wrong.
- **M** Let's try 24, 26. Er, that's, er X and Z. X and Z? No, that can't be right!
- **W** I know. Why don't we try it backwards? 1 is Z, not A. So A is 26, B is 25, C is 24. Like that.
- **M** OK. Let's try. So, 24 is C. 26 is A. CA? What's that?
- **W** Let's go on to the next letter. 13? What's that?
- **M** Er, I know. Why don't we write down all the alphabet and then write down the numbers on top and go backwards with Z as 1, Y as 2, X as 3 and so on.
- **W** Yes. That's a good idea. Let's try that.

Unit 8
Exercise 5: The roaring twenties
- **I** And you were alive then, weren't you?
- **M** Yes, of course, I was very young, but I was alive!
- **I** And you remember the 1920s?
- **M** Oh, yes. I remember, so many things happened. There was something new nearly every day. Everyone started to listen to the radio, and then the first television came out and - cars. Do you know that in 1919 there were 7 million cars in the USA, but by 1929 there were 23 million? Oh, it was fantastic, really. Every week another family got a car. People started flying across the world. Oh, everything changed very quickly. I can remember our family getting its first fridge and washing machine. We thought we were so modern!
- **I** So most people in the States became much richer?
- **M** Well, the rich became very, very rich, and our family did OK at first. But there were still a lot of poor people. Oh, no. Not ... not everyone was rich. But we thought that if we waited a few more years then everyone could, you know er, even the poor people could get rich. But, of course, that didn't happen.
- **I** Do you remember the Wall Street Crash in 1929?
- **M** Oh, yes I do. A terrible time.
- **I** Many families lost everything, didn't they?
- **M** Yes. Our family too. My father's business collapsed. We lost everything. We sold our house, car, even the washing machine went. Oh yes. People lost thousands, millions of dollars.
- **I** And millions of people lost their jobs, didn't they?
- **M** Yes, I think it was 13 or 14 million in America who didn't have jobs in 1930 and millions of others with only part-time jobs. And of course it was the same in Europe. Oh yes it was a ... a terrible end to a decade. Rich one minute, poor the next.

Unit 9
Exercise 3: Green maze

Speaker A
Take the second turning on the left, turn right after the statue, then turn left. Turn left again, and the exit is on your right.

Speaker B
Take the third turning on the right, then turn left. Turn right before the fountain and then take the first turning on your right. Take the second turning on the left and the exit is straight ahead.

Exercise 5: Right or wrong?

Dialogue A
- **M** What do you think about using animals for sport?
- **W** I don't agree with it. It's wrong.
- **M** Why do you say that?
- **W** Well, look at dog fighting, for example. Some people organise dog fights where the dogs kill each other and people do it just to win money on, you know, the best fighter.

M Yes, that's wrong, I agree.
W Even insects. Do you know some people organise fights between insects? They just watch one insect killing another and bet money on the fight.
M Do you think that's wrong? I mean, dogs are one thing but insects? They don't really feel anything, do they?
W That's not true. I think it's wrong to do that to any animal.
M Mhmm?

Dialogue B

M What do you think about this? It says here that in Japan they can make cars which don't need petrol.
W Yeah? What do they use, then?
M I can't explain it exactly, but they use a gas which comes from burning rubbish. I think it's a really good idea. They burn rubbish and then they collect the gas, you know, that comes off, and then use it to make fuel for car engines.
W Well, that sounds a good idea. It's probably cheaper than petrol too.
M Mhmm, mhmm. And it says it gives 25% more power than other fuels.

Dialogue C

M Don't you find them very expensive?
W Yes, they are, but it's much easier than washing them every day. But you're right, they're very expensive, really.
M Babies make so much rubbish, don't they?
W Very true! And all this plastic. It's very difficult to get rid of plastic rubbish, you know.
M Yes, I know. Don't you think they could make them without all that plastic?
W Well, I believe they can now but we haven't got them in the supermarkets yet.

Unit 10

Exercise 3: Booking a place

R Quality Hotel. Good afternoon.
V Oh, hello. I'm telephoning about the Murder Weekends. I'd like to book a room for myself and my husband.
R OK. Now when would you like to come?
V A week on Friday.
R So you want a double room for Friday and Saturday night, the 13th and 14th?
V Yes, thanks.
R What name is it, please?
V Valentine. Mr and Mrs Valentine.
R Mr and Mrs Valentine. Now, would you like a room with a balcony overlooking the garden?
V Er, no thanks. Just a standard room.
R Right. And dinner on Friday evening?
V No, I don't think so. What time do you begin, er with the murder story?
R After dinner on Friday evening. Dinner is at seven thirty, so about eight thirty to nine. It's better to be here by half past eight, really.
V That's fine. We're catching the five thirty train from Cardiff, so we should be in Swindon by about eight. How far are you from the station?
R It's about three miles so if you're not coming by car, you'll need to get a taxi. The hotel has a taxi service from the station. I can book that for you.
V Can I book one now?
R Certainly, madam. What time does your train get into Swindon?
V Five past eight.
R Right. So there'll be a taxi waiting for you and you'll be here about half past eight.
V Half past eight. Fine. And I believe you can hire fancy dress costumes at the hotel?
R That's right. You can hire them when you get here. Do you need costumes for both of you?
V No, just for me. My husband's bringing his own clothes.
R That's fine. So let me just go over the details. A double room for Mr and Mrs Valentine, no balcony. You don't need dinner Friday evening and you want a taxi at the station for five past eight ...

Exercise 5: Going out

Dialogue A

M Look. There's a walk round the city on Sunday morning. Would you like to go?
W What time does it start?
M Half past eight.
W Half past eight? On Sunday morning? Oh, no. That's too early for me. No thanks. I don't think so.
M Oh, come on. Just one Sunday. It looks interesting. It's a historic walk round old churches, and prisons. Why don't you come?
W Oh, all right. Just this once.

Dialogue B

W I've got two tickets for the ballet on Friday. Would you like to come with me?
M Yes. I'd love to. What time does it begin?
W Seven forty five.
M So, shall we meet at seven?
W Yes, where?
M How about outside the theatre?
W Great. See you there at seven on Friday.

Dialogue C

M Oh, er, hello Susan. This is Maurice.
W Hello, Maurice. What do you want?
M Well, er, there's a very good Spanish film on at the moment. I thought, maybe you'd like to come with me one ... one evening.
W No. I'm afraid I can't, Maurice. I'm quite busy at the moment.
M Well, what about next week? We could go then, if you're not too busy.
W No, I'm afraid I haven't got much time in the next three months, Maurice. Sorry. Oh, there's someone at the door. I'll have to go. Bye, Maurice.

TAPESCRIPTS

Exercise 6: Activity weekends

W Right. Can we just take a few minutes to tell you about some of the arrangements this weekend. Maggie?

Ma For those of you who don't know me, my name's Maggie and I'm taking the walkers and sightseers. On Saturday morning we're going to the castle and gardens. We're meeting outside and we're going by minibus to the castle - leaving at ten. After we've looked round the castle and gardens we're walking back along footpaths and country roads. It's about 15 kilometres so bring comfortable shoes. It's not a difficult walk but it is quite long and it can be very muddy.

W Thanks, Maggie. Ian?

I OK. Well, on Saturday morning I'm taking the pottery class. This is a beginners class, so don't worry if you've never done it before. We're starting after breakfast at nine thirty in room 8. The class will last all morning, and if you're very keen, there's another class in the afternoon.

W Thanks, Ian. And now, Chris.

C Right. Well, for you sports people, we've got golf all day Sunday. We're meeting outside in the car park at ten and we're walking from here to the golf course. It's about a couple of miles so we'll be on the course at about ten thirty. And one more thing. I'm sorry but there's no parachuting today. I'm afraid it's too windy and they're not flying today. If it's better tomorrow we'll organise something then. I'll tell you about that at breakfast tomorrow. Right. That's it, I think.

Unit 11

Exercise 2: Youth enterprise

Part 1

I Youth Enterprise is a great opportunity for you and other school students. It's a chance for you to start a business for yourself while you are still at school. You work out your own ideas, make your own decisions and work together, as a business team. And don't forget, at the end there is a competition to find the best Youth Enterprise business in the country. The winners receive a cheque for £1,000, and there are two other prizes of £750 and £500 for the second and third teams. Now, are there any questions?

Part 2

S1 How many schools are there in the scheme?

I Well, last year there were about 2,000 schools in the scheme.

S2 And were they successful? I mean, did anyone make a profit?

I Oh, yes. There are some students here who had two very successful businesses.

S3 How much money do we get to start the business?

I You don't get any money. You have to find all the money yourselves. That's part of the competition.

S4 And you said we work in teams. How many people are there in a team?

I That depends. If there is a large group of you who can work together, then you can have a large team. But, er, if you prefer to work with a couple of friends, that's OK. It really depends on you and what you think will work the best. And we suggest you spend about two hours a week on the scheme. We don't want you to miss your other school work.

S5 And can we get advice from anyone?

I Yes. There is a teacher in each school who can help you. If you think it's helpful the teacher can ask one of our advisers to come to the school to answer more questions. And now I'd like to introduce Brian and David who can tell you about the business they started last year.

Part 3

I So, any questions for Brian and David?

S1 Er, what did you make?

B We made two things. The first thing was ties. Very colourful ties were really popular last year at school so we thought that was a good idea ...

D Yes, and the other thing was exam revision papers. We looked at a lot of exam papers from past years and made lots of very simple revision sheets in different subjects. They sold like hot cakes.

S2 How many ties did you sell?

D So far we've sold 400 and we have got orders for more.

S3 And how much profit did you make?

B With the ties and the revision papers together we made £500 profit last year.

S4 How much did the revision papers cost?

B £1.50 each. There were about 18 pages in each little booklet.

S5 How many students were there in the team?

D Er, eight. No, nine.

S1 And did you find that once you'd ...?

Exercise 6: Sympathising and congratulating

Part 1

Dialogue A

M How are things?

W Not too good, I'm afraid. Last week I only had ten customers. I made a loss of about £500.

M Oh, dear. I'm very sorry to hear that.

Dialogue B

W Hey, I've just won first prize in a competition!

M That's fantastic! What did you win?

W A holiday in the Bahamas.

M How wonderful!

Dialogue C

M I passed!

W Oh well done! Congratulations!

M Thanks. I got 68%.

Dialogue D

W What's wrong?

M Oh, we can't go the concert.

W Why not?

M They've sold out of tickets.

W Oh, no. What a pity. Never mind. We can go somewhere else.

Part 2

1. I passed my driving test.
2. We can't go on our picnic. The weather's too bad.
3. I've just won £700 in the lottery.
4. I got the job.
5. I'm afraid I didn't pass. I only got 30%.
6. I'm sorry I can't come tomorrow. My mother's in hospital.
7. We sold twelve paintings this week. We've made about £2,500.
8. I'm afraid we had to close down our business. We couldn't pay back the bank and we were making a loss.

Unit 12

Exercise 4: Different traditions

I So, what are you going to wear?
W Oh, it's a beautiful dress. The material came from India - my Aunt sent it to me. It's red and green with gold threads running through it. My mother's going to make it into a sari.
I You're not going to wear white then?
W Oh, no. Indian women can't wear white for weddings. In Indian tradition white means death, so it's for funerals.
I Oh, I see. So what's the usual colour for wedding dresses?
W Red or pink often with some green, as well. Red is a very important colour for weddings.
I Yes, I've seen women with their hands painted red. Is that henna?
W Yes it is. We use henna to paint patterns all over our hands.
I Are you going to do that?
W Oh yes. Well, my friends are going to paint them for me the night before the wedding.
I Mhmm. I think it looks lovely.
W Yes. And gold - that's another important colour at Indian weddings.
I Oh?
W Oh yes. My dress is going to have gold in it and I'm going to wear lots of gold jewellery, for example.
I Is that usual?
W Yes. The bride's parents buy her gold before the wedding. And we give presents that are gold too.
I What do you mean - you give presents? I thought the bride receives the presents not gives the presents?
W Well, it's Indian tradition. The bride's family gives presents to the bridegroom's mother, sister, uncle. Oh, all sorts of people get presents.
I What kind of presents?
W Jewellery, gold usually or sometimes money.
I So, you're going to buy lots of jewellery in the next few weeks for your husband's family?
W Yes, me and my Mum are going shopping tomorrow.
I I hope you're going to get some presents, too.
W Oh, yes! We get gold and money, too.

Exercise 6: Do you agree?

Dialogue A

W1 I think 18 is too young to get married.
M Yes, definitely.
W2 Well, I disagree. I got married at 17 and we're very happy.

Dialogue B

W I don't believe in marriage. I think if you love each other you don't need to get married.
M Oh, I don't think so. If you're married, you stay together longer.
W Yes, but if you love each other you stay together, too.
M No. I don't agree. It's not the same.

Dialogue C

W1 I think it's better to get married when you're between 25 and 30.
W2 Yes, I think so, too.
W1 You're not ready when you're young and you need to meet a lot of people before you choose someone you want to marry.
W2 Yes, that's right.

Dialogue D

M Well, I want to marry someone a few years younger than me.
W What? You think it's better for the man to be a bit older than the woman?
M Yes, I think so.
W No. It doesn't matter which one is older.

Unit 13

Exercise 2: Experienced travellers

Dialogue A

M Well, I know that everyone goes to see the pyramids but what else do you think we should see?
W Oh, in Cairo you should go to the museum. And I really enjoyed going round the mosques. Some of them are very beautiful.
M What else did you like?
W Oh, shopping in the bazaar. That was great. You should definitely go to the bazaar. There are some wonderful things and you sit down at the stall, drink tea and talk about how much you want to pay and ...
M What? They don't have fixed prices?
W Not really. You should bargain for things.
M Oh, I'm not sure I'd be very good at that. But what about food? What's Egyptian food like?
W Good. I like it. You should try some of the Egyptian restaurants and don't eat in your hotel all the time.
M Mhmm. So, what about the rest of the country ...

Dialogue B

W So when do you think is the best time to go?
M Well, winter's no good because it's too cold and the days are very short, you know, it gets dark in the middle of the afternoon. The best time is summer - between May and September. It's lovely then.

TAPESCRIPTS

W And where did you stay when you went? In youth hostels?
M Mhmm.
W What are they like?
M Oh they are fantastic over there. There's a hostel in Stockholm that's in an old sailing ship.
W Really?
M Yes. But don't just go along without booking. You should always book in advance because they get really busy in summer.
W And can I book from here?
M Yes. Er, I've got the address of the tourist board somewhere ...

Dialogue C

M And do I need a visa?
W Yes, you must have a visa. And you should apply about two months before you go.
M So you think I should go at the end of summer?
W Yes. I think September and October are the best months. It's still warm, it's usually dry and sunny and the trees and parks are beautiful in October.
M So what clothes do I need then?
W Oh, cotton trousers and shirts, a sweater for the evenings and maybe one jacket but it's quite warm in the daytime.
M But was it difficult finding your way around? I mean, how can you read the signs?
W There are a lot of signs in the Roman alphabet in the big cities and in the tourist places they have signs in English. But people are very friendly and helpful and a lot of people can speak some English ...

Exercise 6: Money matters

Dialogue A

M Can I have £1,000 worth of traveller's cheques, please?
W Certainly, sir. Do you want the cheques in US dollars?
M Yes, please. And I'd like to change £500 into Hong Kong dollars, as well.
W Right. Could you sign here, please and I'll get you the Hong Kong dollars.

Dialogue B

W Here's my room key. Er, how much do I owe you?
M Thank you, madam. I'll just get your bill. That's 480 francs.
W Can I pay by credit card?
M I'm afraid we don't accept credit cards, just cash or cheques.
W Oh dear. Well, can you cash me these traveller's cheques, please?
M Certainly, madam. How much would you like?
W Er, £200 sterling in French francs.
M Right.

Dialogue C

W Hello. Can you change these German marks into pounds for me?
M Yes. I can change the notes but I'm afraid we can't change coins.
W Oh. Well, where can I change them?
M You can't change them - use them for your next holiday!

Unit 14
Exercise 4: Talented children

I And is it very difficult for the teachers, having a boy in the class who's so talented at maths?
W Well, it is in many ways. I mean, we've taught him everything we can - in maths. You see, he's only nine and he's passed exams for sixteen-year-olds.
I Really?
W Yes, but fortunately, his father helps us a lot. He was a maths teacher himself and he gives Ricardo extra maths problems to do. And his father has bought him a computer, so he can do a lot of extra work at home.
I Do you think that his parents and his teachers push him too hard?
W No, I don't think so. You see, he loves maths, and when he's finished one problem, he's looking for the next.

I Stephen is a very special boy, isn't he?
M Yes, he is. In many ways he doesn't have the normal abilities for a boy of his age. It's very difficult for him to read and write, for example.
I And he's sixteen now?
M That's right, and many eight-year-old boys can do much more than he can but, of course, he has a special talent.
I In drawing.
M Yes, he has always been fantastic at it. Stephen can look at any building for about five minutes and then draw it perfectly.
I Tell us about some of the drawings he's done.
M Well, he's drawn some very complex buildings likes the Doge's Palace in Venice. He's drawn the Gum department store in Moscow and the Kremlin, and they are wonderful. Famous art experts have looked at the drawings and said that Stephen's an excellent artist.
I And he just looks at these buildings for a few minutes and then draws them?
M That's right. It's very strange, isn't it. He has such a special talent in one thing, but he finds other things difficult.

Exercise 6: Checking understanding

Dialogue A

M Do you mean he scored over 1,000 goals?
W Yes, 1,200 I think.
M And he won three World Cup medals?
W Yes - in 1958, 1962 and 1970.
M Amazing.

Dialogue B

W What did you say? He wrote music when he was six years old?
M That's right.
W I can't believe it.
M It's true.
W And let me just check this. He wrote 1,000 pieces of music.
M Yes.
W Phew!

Unit 15

Exercise 4: Identical twins

- **I** Now, Martin and Peter, you're identical twins, aren't you?
- **M** Yes.
- **P** That's right.
- **I** And did your parents always know who was Martin and who was Peter?
- **P** Yes, our parents did, but other people didn't. You know, I pretended I was Martin and he pretended he was me - especially with the teachers at school.
- **I** I can imagine. And Martin, you were born first, weren't you?
- **M** Yes, I was. Ten minutes before Peter.
- **I** Do you think that's important?
- **M** Yes, I'm bossier than my brother, more aggressive. I like to be, you know, always the first.
- **I** Is that true, Peter?
- **P** Yes, it is. I was always the quiet one and Martin was noisier than me as a child. And he liked to be the first in the class, you know, get the best marks.
- **I** But you're different now, aren't you?
- **M** Er, mhmm, yes. But I think Peter is still quieter than me.
- **I** And you both had problems learning to speak, didn't you?
- **P** Yes. It was difficult for our parents, really.
- **M** Yes, you see, we had our own language. We didn't speak, you know, normally. We spoke in a special language to each other.
- **I** So you and Peter could understand each other but nobody else could understand you?
- **P** That's right. We were together all the time, so we spoke our own private language and we didn't need to learn to speak properly.
- **I** Yes, I believe a lot of twins do this, have their own private language. Can you remember any of the language now?
- **M** No, but Mum says we didn't say 'mum' or 'mummy', we called her 'Gobu'. My dad was 'Lotta' and we always said 'tek' if we wanted to say 'no'. I wish we had a cassette of us talking when we were babies. It would be really interesting now.

Unit 16

Exercise 4: Looking to the future

Dialogue A
- **M** It says here that in fifty years time most people will work from home and we'll send our work to a central office by computer.
- **W** Oh, I hope not.
- **M** Why? I think it's quite a good idea to work from home.
- **W** Oh, no. I don't think so. I like working with other people, not on my own.

Dialogue B
- **W** Listen to this. 'By the year 2000 most homes will be heated by solar energy.'
- **M** I hope so. I think it's the cheapest and cleanest form of energy.
- **W** Yes, I think so too.

Dialogue C
- **W** Do you know that in a hundred years time we'll all have robots to do the housework?
- **M** Well, I hope so.
- **W** Great idea, isn't it?
- **M** What about our jobs? I hope we won't have robots to do our jobs as well.
- **W** Oh no, I don't think so. Do you?
- **M** Well, I hope not.

Exercise 6: Food for the future

Good morning. Today I'm going to talk about food - food in the future. Now, maybe some of you know this, but about two thirds of the world is covered by water - oceans, seas, lakes and so on. Two thirds of our planet is water, but most of our food comes from the land. Only two or three per cent of our food comes from oceans and seas. Now, we won't have enough food for everyone until we use the world's water better, more efficiently. Look at this illustration here. I want to show you how fishing could be much better in the future. We might have automatic fishing boats, for example, with computers and satellites telling the boats where to fish. But if we take out more fish from the sea we'll need to put something back. It won't be possible just to take more from the sea. So we'll have lots more fish farms producing fish all the time, to put the fish back into the sea.

Then there are vegetables. It's possible to have large vegetable farms on the sea. Like this illustration here. Vegetables on raised platforms in the sea. They won't use salt water of course, they'll use the water that comes off the sea in water vapour, as the sea gets warm.

Now, what about the desert? So much of our land is desert. But look at my illustrations of these large domes in the desert with pipes bringing water. The plants will get plenty of sun and the domes will keep the water inside. And then, who knows, we might have robots to plant, pick and pack the plants - a type of robotic farmer. And all these things will run on solar energy, of course. We will have solar energy everywhere in a few years time. Any questions so far ...?

Unit 17

Exercise 4: Adventurous ideas

- **I** Sally, you've been in the travel business for a long time. How did it all start?
- **S** Oh, I suppose when I was a child. You see, we lived in many different countries, er, first Britain, then Belgium, France, Spain and Switzerland.
- **I** So you speak quite a lot of languages?

TAPESCRIPTS

S Yes, French, Spanish, German and English. So, you see, I've been a traveller for a long time.
I So you decided to sell unusual holidays, adventure holidays, really.
S That's right.
I Can you tell us about some of the holidays we can get through your agency?
S Yes. Well, there's a very interesting holiday in Zambia, for example, where you can stay in an animal conservation park.
I Mm. That's a park where they look after wild animals?
S Yes. There are some scientists who work there all the time studying the animals.
I What kind of animals can you find there?
S Oh, er, elephants, lions, er, blue monkey, zebras. And people can stay in the park in tents and watch the scientists at work. We organise walks, river trips, fishing trips, bird watching trips, it's a fantastic holiday.
I Are all your holidays outside Europe?
S Oh no. There's a very good holiday in France, for example. We go hot-air ballooning there. But you have to get up very early in the morning for that, when it's not too windy.
I That sounds wonderful. How long do you stay up in the balloon?
S Oh, about an hour. And everyone can do one or two flights a day.
I I'd love to go on both those holidays. But aren't your holidays all rather expensive?
S No. We have a very good holiday in Sweden, for example. It's a rafting holiday. When you get to Sweden, someone shows you how to make your own raft from tree logs. You bring your own tent, we give you a map of rivers in the area and you travel along the rivers in the raft - where you want - and camp on the riverside. That's a very cheap holiday.

Exercise 6: Not good enough

R Hello, reception, can I help you?
W Yes. This is Mrs Jameson, room 306. I'd like to speak to the manager, please.
R Just one moment, madam, I'll put you through.
M Hello, this is Mr Saville, the manager.
W Ah, this is Mrs Jameson, room 306. I'm calling about my room. I'd like to make a complaint.
M Oh dear, is something wrong?
W Yes, I'm afraid there is. I am not satisfied with my room. It's in a mess. The bed isn't made, there are dirty ashtrays on the table ...
M I am terribly sorry, madam, I'll send someone up right away.
W And there's another thing. The bathroom is dirty and there's a big spider in the washbasin.
M I really must apologise for all this, madam. Let me offer you another room with a 20% discount.
W Well, that'll be fine. Thank you.

Unit 18

Exercise 2: In the family

Part 1

Romance isn't only for young people, you know. Me and George are very romantic, really. We've been married for about six months now. After we got married we wanted, you know, a special holiday. I suppose it's a honeymoon, really. Anyway, we're going to Australia to visit my sister and George's son and grandchildren. His son has been in Australia since 1980, so he hasn't seen him since then. And my sister - well, I haven't seen her since 1962. I mean, we've written, but we haven't met since she went out there. So, anyway, we've planned this big holiday.

Part 2

You see, my daughter's husband died just after the little girl was born and it was very difficult for her, so I've lived here with them since then. I look after my granddaughter during the day while her mum goes to college. She's studying nursing. She was a nurse before, but she hasn't worked for a long time now and, well - so many things have changed since she stopped work. And Robert, that's my grandson, he's been a big help to his mum since his dad died, but he's still at school ...

Part 3

Oh, no. I don't want to live with anyone. My daughter's always asking me to go and live with them, but - no. I want to stay here. I've lived here for fifty odd years, I don't want to move now. I like cooking, reading ... no, I'm fine on my own. I'm never sick. In fact, I haven't been near a doctor for twenty years. Oh, I suppose I might get married. There are a couple of women after me, you know. But, no, I think I'm better off on my own. I can do what I want, you know, please myself.

Exercise 5: A helping hand

Dialogue A

W1 Would you like a seat?
W2 Oh, thank you, that's very kind of you.
W1 Here, let me take your shopping.
W2 Thanks a lot. It's quite heavy.

Dialogue B

M Shall I help you across the street?
W No thanks, I'm quite all right.
M It's no trouble. It's very busy right now.
W I'm fine, really, I can manage by myself.

Dialogue C

M1 Can you manage?
M2 I don't think I can reach those biscuits. They're too high up.
M1 Here. Let me get them for you.
M2 Thanks very much. That's a big help.

Unit 19

Exercise 4: Five Field Kono

W Do you know Five Field Kono?
M No, I don't think so. What kind of game is it?
W It's a Korean board game. You play on a square board divided into 16 squares, four across, four down.
M Yes ...
W You don't have to have a special board. You can use a piece of paper, like this ...
M Mhmm.
W Now each player has seven pieces. You can use buttons or coins, but it's better if they're different colours. One colour for each player.
M OK. Where do you have to put the pieces?
W Well, I put five across the bottom, one on each corner of the squares, like this. And the other two at the sides, one on each side. Then you have to do the same with the other seven pieces at the top. Five across the top and one at each side.
M Like this?
W That's right.
M And how do you play?
W Well, you have to get your pieces to the other side. I have to get my pieces to your side and you have to get your pieces to my side.
M What? You have to move along the lines?
W No, you have to move diagonally across the squares - backwards or forwards.
M Forwards or backwards? Why backwards?
W Because you have to move a piece every time. If you can't go forwards, you have to go backwards. And you can't move if there's another piece already there.
M OK, let's have a game then.
W Right, you start.
M Is it better to go first?
W I'm not telling you. You'll find out when you play.

Exercise 6: Persuading

M1 Who's for a game of cards?
W1 No thanks, I'm no good at cards.
M1 Oh, come on. We'll play something easy.
M2 I'm not playing with you, you always cheat.
M1 Cheat? No, I don't! I'm just lucky.
W2 Huh, you usually win, and it's not always good luck. No, I don't feel like it anyway ...
M1 OK. OK. No cheating. Come on, let's have just one game.
W1 Oh, all right then, just one game.
M1 How about you two? Go on. A quick game. You can choose what we play.
W1 Go on then, we'll play. But just one game.
M1 Right, I'll shuffle. You say which game you want.

Unit 20

Exercise 4: Sea zoo

I When did this Sea Zoo open?
M About three years ago. Sea zoos are very popular now, especially with children. You see, children who don't live near the sea never normally see these creatures. But now they can come here, see lots of sea creatures and plants, read about them and even touch some of them.
I Which ones are the most popular?
M Oh, the sharks, I think. Children know about sharks and they're usually afraid of them. So they like to see them close up, you know, to see their teeth - behind the glass screen, of course. And the lobsters. I think because they can pick them up and look closely at them. Lobsters are very strange looking things, with their long pincers at the front. And children sometimes know that lobsters will eat each other if they're hungry, so some children watch the lobsters for hours, waiting to see if this will happen.
I Oh dear. I don't think I'd like that.
M And another popular one is the octopus. You know an octopus will change colour if it's in danger. It can change to match it's surroundings so that the attackers can't see it.
I I didn't know that.
M Oh yes, it's wonderful to watch. And, of course, it's such a strange looking creature with its large eyes, long arms and rubbery body.
I I know that octopuses will release a black liquid in the water if something attacks them.
M That's right. If something attacks an octopus it will shoot off at a great speed and let out the black liquid. The black liquid makes a kind of cloud behind the octopus so the attacker can't see very well and the liquid also contains a chemical with a strong smell. The attacker will follow the smell of the chemical and not of the octopus itself.
I It's a very good defence, isn't it.
M Yes, it is. And another thing people often don't know about octopuses is that when the female lays her eggs she will guard them for weeks and as soon as the eggs hatch, the female will die.
I Really? ...

Exercise 6: Strange pets

Dialogue A

W There was a woman on the radio talking about her pet spiders.
M What? She keeps spiders as pets?
W Yes, it was really interesting.
M Ugh! No, not spiders.
W Why, what's wrong?
M I can't stand spiders, I'm terrified of them.

Dialogue B

M We're looking after my cousin's snake.
W What? In your house?
M Yes, but it's in a cage.
W Oh no.
M Come and see.
W No, really. I'm scared of snakes.
M It's asleep.
W No. I couldn't look at it.

PROJECTS

Project 1: Shopping chart of students' host town.

Intended readership: Students themselves, other classes in their school, their local library or tourist office.

Aim of project: Groups/pairs of students must use 'clues' distributed by the teacher to find out where a product comes from and use the information as a basis for comparing shops and services in their town and contributing to a class chart.

STAGE 1: **Before coming to class**
1 Collect labels, price tags, brochures or small items from a range of local shops, for example:
travel agent, coffee shop, restaurant, clothes shop, shoe shop book/record shop, souvenir/local product shop. You may wish to select alternatives, depending on your location. The students must guess where their 'clue' has come from, so the clues should not be too obvious.

STAGE 2: **Planning**
1 Ensure that students understand the aim of the project, ie that each group has to find out (a) where their clue has come from, (b) more about the shop selling the item and (c) compare with other similar shops (the number compared will depend on the location). Finally, students should use this information to fill in a chart, like the example opposite.
2 Put students in groups of 3 or 4, or pairs, depending on the size of the class. Ask them to select a clue.
3 Let groups/pairs discuss where they think their clue has come from.
4 Groups/pairs discuss the information they will require from the various shops. Look at the chart opposite with the groups, for examples of the sort of information they may want.

STAGE 3: **Preparation**
1 Each group prepares its contribution. Though some of this will have to be done outside of class time, provide them with any help that they need. Be careful, though, not to 'take over' the project.

STAGE 4: **Putting together the chart**
Students work together to plan the layout of their chart and put together their contributions, 'editing' them if necessary. Students decide if/how they want to adapt the format opposite.

STAGE 5: **The final product**
If the chart is small in size, make copies for the students. If the chart is larger, ensure that the students have a record of their contribution. Also, make copies for other classes, or future classes.

FURTHER ACTIVITIES BASED ON THIS PROJECT:
1 **'Best of...' guide**
Students select the 'best' shop in each category and create a 'Best of...' chart/guide.
2 **Shopping map**
Students create a shopping map of their town. They can draw a larger-size, tourist map of the town and insert symbols, representing the various shops, on it. Students can write a couple of lines on each shop and make a key to the symbols on the map.
3 **Tourist walks**
Students write the text and map for tourist shopping walks of the town.

COFFEE SHOPS

Name: Street:	Ken's Koffee Shop 10 Castle Street	Susan's Place 3 Green Square	The Coffee Pot 92 Bridge Road
Tel no: Items sold:	222 209 tea coffee cakes pastries	236 549 tea coffee cakes chips	205 883 tea coffee cakes salad baked potatoes
Prices:	tea/coffee 50/60p cakes 40-80p	tea/coffee 40/50p cakes 40-60p chips 50p	tea/coffee 45/55p cakes 40-60p salads around £1.00
Quality:	very good	quite good	excellent - baked potatoes are delicious
Other comments:	The cakes are very good quality. So is the coffee. It is more expensive than Susan's Place.	Not as good as Ken's Koffee Shop, but cheaper.	Food very nice and prices very reasonable.

CLOTHES SHOPS

Name: Street:	The Wardrobe 40 The Parade	Belinda's 63 Old Street	Prima Bridge Shopping Centre
Tel no: Items sold:	259 002 clothes	306 446 clothes	393 5050 clothes/food household items
Prices:	1 blouse £25	1 blouse £70	1 blouse £12.99
Quality:	quite good	very good	good
Other comments:	The clothes were medium price and quite good quality.	Very good quality clothes but expensive.	Lots of cheap good quality clothes.

PROJECTS

Project 2: Family tree

Intended readership: Students and teacher in the class and for individual student reference once the course has finished.

Aim of project: Each student draws his/her own family tree, interviews other students in the group about members of their family to complete Personal History Sheets and uses the Sheets to write profiles of other students' relatives.

STAGE 1: **Before coming to class**
Make 2/3 copies of the Personal History Sheet opposite for each student in the class. Complete a Personal History Sheet for a member of your family, as an example.

STAGE 2: **Planning**
1 Put students in groups of 3 or 4.
2 Distribute copies of the Personal History Sheet to each group member.
3 Ensure that each student understands the aim of the project. Students look at and discuss the vocabulary in the Personal History Sheet (show them your copy as an example) and look at the example family tree opposite.
4 Explain that the students can alter/adapt the Personal History Sheet if they wish.
5 When groups have agreed on their versions of the Personal History Sheet, go over the questions they might ask to complete the form, e.g. *What is his/her relationship to you? What is his/her name? When was he/she born?* (**Not** *What is his/her date of birth?*)

STAGE 3: **Preparation**
1 Each student draws his/her own family tree.
2 Students interview other members of their groups about members of their families. Students may like to interview several members of their group, but ensure that each student in the group interviews and is interviewed at least once.
3 Each student uses the information in the Personal History Sheet to write a profile of the interviewee's family member.

STAGE 4: **The final product**
1 Each student has a copy of his/her family tree for reference, at least one completed Personal History Sheet for a member of his/her family, and a profile of a family member to put in his/her file.
2 Copies of family trees can go on display in the classroom.

FURTHER ACTIVITY BASED ON THIS PROJECT:
1 Students write about their family origins, including where members of the family, eg grandparents, came from and when.

PROJECTS

Personal History Sheet

Relationship to you ....
Name ....
Nationality .... Occupation ....
Date of birth .... Place of birth ....

Married to ....
Nationality .... Occupation ....
Date of birth .... Place of birth ....
Children ....
....

Additional information ....
....
....
....

The Robinson Family

PROJECTS

Project 3: End of term/course party

Aim of project: Students organise and host a party.

STAGE 1: **Before coming to class**
1 Get several large sheets of paper with coloured pens for students to make posters with.

STAGE 2: **Planning**
1 Tell students that they are going to organise a party. Decide at the outset if it is going to be a party for the class or a party for the school.
2 Students decide on a theme for the party. For example, they might want to choose one of the themes from their coursebook, like a Twenties theme, or a Life in the Future theme. If the party is to be fancy dress, they might want to come dressed as unusual animals.
3 Impose a budget. Get each student to contribute whatever seems reasonable for your class. This is the money for food and drinks. Students decide how they're going to cater for the party with this money.
4 Put students in groups to organise: the food, the posters and invitations, the decorations, the music, etc.
5 If the students in the class are younger, suggest party games, like *I spy*, *Alibi* and *Spelling Bingo*.

STAGE 3: **Preparation**
1 Students in their groups prepare for the party. Give advice or suggestions as necessary, (you might like to provide the raw materials for the poster or recipes for the party food, for example) but remember that this is the students' party.

STAGE 4: **Final product**
1 If the party is fancy dress, give a prize for the best costume. Otherwise, give prizes for the best dancer, best poster, party dish, etc.
2 The teacher or one of the students can be in charge of taking photographs.

FURTHER ACTIVITY BASED ON THIS PROJECT:
A 'Course party' booklet
Containing:
  i) a collage of photographs taken at the party with captions
  ii) a book of recipes for the food prepared for the party
  iii) directions for party games played at the party
  iv) suggestions for themes for a party
  v) copies of invitations and posters
  vi) a copy of the menu/food offered at the party
Each student should have a copy of the booklet to take away with him/her.

Twenties PARTY

Date: 21st June
Time: 8pm
Place: The school hall
Dress: 20s
BRING A FRIEND!

Irregular verbs

Infinitive	Simple Past	Past Participle	Infinitive	Simple Past	Past Participle
be	was/were	been	make	made	made
become	became	become	may	might	—
begin	began	begun	mean	meant	meant
bite	bit	bitten	meet	met	met
blow	blew	blown	pay	paid	paid
break	broke	broken	put	put	put
bring	brought	brought	read	read	read
build	built	built	ride	rode	ridden
burn	burned/burnt	burnt/burned	ring	rung	rang
buy	bought	bought	rise	rose	risen
can	could	been able	run	ran	run
catch	caught	caught	say	said	said
choose	chose	chosen	see	saw	seen
come	came	come	sell	sold	sold
cost	cost	cost	send	sent	sent
cut	cut	cut	set	set	set
dig	dug	dug	sew	sewed	sewn
do	did	done	shake	shook	shaken
draw	drew	drawn	shave	shaved	shaved
dream	dreamt/dreamed	dreamt/dreamed	shine	shone	shone
drink	drank	drunk	shoot	shot	shot
drive	drove	driven	show	showed	shown
eat	ate	eaten	shut	shut	shut
fall	fell	fallen	sing	sang	sung
feed	fed	fed	sink	sank	sunk
feel	felt	felt	sit	sat	sat
fight	fought	fought	sleep	slept	slept
find	found	found	smell	smelt/smelled	smelt/smelled
fly	flew	flown	speak	spoke	spoken
forget	forgot	forgotten	speed	sped/speeded	sped/speeded
forgive	forgave	forgiven	spell	spelt	spelt
freeze	froze	frozen	spend	spent	spent
get	got	got	spread	spread	spread
give	gave	given	stand	stood	stood
go	went	gone	steal	stole	stolen
grow	grew	grown	stick	stuck	stuck
hang	hung	hung	sting	stang	stung
have	have	have	sweep	swept	swept
hear	heard	heard	swell	swelled	swollen
hit	hit	hit	swim	swam	swum
hold	held	held	take	took	taken
hurt	hurt	hurt	teach	taught	taught
keep	kept	kept	tear	tore	torn
know	knew	known	tell	told	told
lay	laid	laid	think	thought	thought
lead	led	led	throw	threw	thrown
lean	leant/leaned	leant/leaned	understand	understood	understood
learn	learnt/learned	learnt/learned	wake	woke	woken
leave	left	left	wear	wore	worn
lend	lent	lent	win	won	won
let	let	let	wind	wound	wound
light	lit	lit	write	wrote	written
lose	lost	lost			

Wordlist

*The numbers following each word in the list refer to the word's occurrence in the **Student's and Practice Book**. Bold type denotes the unit and normal type the exercise number in which the word may be found.*

Word	Ref	Word	Ref	Word	Ref
(big) help	18.2	beetle	9.5	cheese	5.5
(chest of) drawers	2.5	better	15.2	cheque	11.2
(fifty) odd years	18.2	birdwatching	17.4	chess	19.1
(in a) mess	17.6	biscuits	5.2	chicken	5.2
(more) aggressive	15.4	bite	20.2	chips	5.2
(the) same (as)	14.4	block (of flats)	2.2	chocolate	5.1
(weight) training	6.6	board	19.2	choice	17.2
abbreviation	12.7	boarding card	13.3	cinema	1.5
abroad	6.2	book (a lesson)	3.6	circus	6.4
accept	14.2	book	13.2	classical (music)	1.5
accommodation	17.2	bother	20.2	climate	18.4
active	4.2	bottom	19.4	close up	20.4
address	1.2	Brazilian	1.2	closer	15.2
adventurous	17.4	bride	12.4	cloud	20.4
advice	3.2	bridegroom	12.4	cockroach	20.3
adviser	11.2	burglar	4.6	code	7.5
afford	12.2	business	11.1	coffee table	2.4
afraid	20.1	busker	6.6	coins	13.6
age	6.7	butter	5.5	collapsed	8.6
agency	1.2	buttons	19.4	colleague	1.1
album	12.7	by hand	16.1	collecting	3.2
alcohol	18.4	by myself	2.2	college	18.2
alive	8.5	cage	20.6	colour	12.4
alphabet	7.5	calm	20.5	come near	20.3
ancient	10.5	camp	17.4	communicating	7.1
animal	17.4	camping	17.2	communist	8.4
anyone	7.2	campsites	17.2	company	11.4
architecture	10.5	can't stand	16.2	compartment	4.4
area	16.2	caravan	2.1	competition	11.2
army	6.2	caravans	17.2	complex	14.4
arrest	15.5	career	6.2	computer	7.2
arrested	4.4	carrots	5.1	concert	14.2
artist	14.4	cartoon	8.6	confidence	11.1
assistant	4.2	case (s)	4.2	construction company	16.2
astonished	14.2	cash a cheque	13.6	container	9.2
at home	15.2	cat	20.3	continue	19.2
attack	20.2	cell	8.2	cook	6.4
attacker	20.4	central heating	2.2	corner	19.2
autobiography	14.2	century	8.7	correct (v)	19.2
automatic fishing boats	16.6	cereal	5.2	cost of living	13.5
backwards	19.4	ceremony	12.2	costume	10.2
bad weather	6.6	certain	16.3	cotton	13.2
balcony	10.2	certificate	12.2	country	4.2
bananas	5.1	chains	8.2	cousin	2.6
bargain (v)	13.2	change colour	20.4	crab	20.3
barrel	2.4	change money	13.6	creature	20.2
bathrooms	2.2	character	7.5	credit card	13.6
bazaar	13.2	characteristics	20.3	crowds	20.5
beaches	17.2	charge	11.2	customer	11.4
beans	19.2	cheap	15.6	dancer	5.5
bedrooms	2.2	cheat (v)	19.6	dangerous	6.6
bees	4.2	Cheerio!	1.1	day(s) off	6.6

WORDLIST

dead	4.4	family tree	2.6	hobby	10.2
deaf	14.2	famous	4.2	holiday	17.1
death	12.4	fancy dress	10.2	home	2.1
decade	8.7	fantastic	13.2	honeymoon	18.2
decisions	11.2	farming	16.6	horseman	18.4
delicious	15.6	fashion	8.6	hostels	17.2
depressed	5.2	fashionable	1.2	house	2.1
desert	16.6	fat	5.1	houseboat	2.1
detective	4.1	fear	20.6	housework	16.4
diagonally	19.4	female	20.4	huge	2.2
dice	19.2	festival	15.2	humidity	17.2
difficult	6.2	financial market	8.6	hunting	17.2
diplomas	6.4	finger	4.4	idea	11.1
directions	9.3	first name	1.2	ideal	1.2
dirty	17.6	fishing	17.2	identical	15.2
disappeared	4.4	fitted wardrobes	2.5	immediately	8.2
disaster	8.6	flat	2.1	in/out of danger	20.4
discos	1.5	flexible	6.2	infant	18.1
disposable	9.6	floor (of a building)	16.2	injured	20.2
distance	3.2	foothills	17.7	intelligent	4.1
disturb	20.2	forwards	19.4	interests	1.2
domes	16.6	freaks	15.2	interior designer	2.5
draughts	19.1	free time	10.1	invested	11.4
drawing	14.4	French	1.2	jealous	10.2
dream	3.4	fresh	5.2	jewellery	12.4
drivers	3.2	fridge	8.5	jewels	8.6
driving licence	6.4	fried	5.2	join	6.2
earn	6.6	frightening	20.6	journey	3.2
easier	15.2	funding	11.4	juice	5.6
economics	8.6	funeral	12.4	keen on	6.2
education	11.1	gambling	18.4	kidnapped	4.6
egg	20.4	game	19.1	killer	10.2
elderly	18.1	garden	2.2	lakes	17.2
electric	9.2	genius	14.5	lay	20.4
electricity	2.2	get on/off	4.4	leaflet	9.2
embarrassed	5.2	glass	11.4	leave alone	20.2
emigrated	8.2	gloves	4.4	left-over	5.2
energetic	4.2	goals	14.5	leisure	10.1
energy	5.1	gold	8.6	lemon	5.6
engine	9.6	golf course	17.2	letter	7.5
English	1.2	government	4.2	lions	20.2
entertainer	6.6	graduate	11.4	lip-read	14.2
entertainment	8.6	grandchildren	18.2	liquid	20.2
environment	9.1	grandfather	2.6	literature	4.2
equal	12.5	grandmother	2.6	litter	9.1
escaped	8.2	guard	20.4	load	13.4
events	8.5	guide	10.6	loan	11.4
exam (revision) papers	11.2	habits	4.2	lobster	20.4
exams	6.4	hard	6.2	locked	8.2
excellent	14.4	hatch	20.4	long life	18.4
exercise	5.2	health	3.1	look for	9.2
experience	6.7	healthy	5.1	lost	20.2
experience(d)	6.4	heavy	15.5	luck	11.1
experts	7.2	heights	16.2	luxurious	17.2
explanation	4.4	hide	20.3	mad	16.2
expressions	1.1	high street	15.2	magic tricks	8.2
extra	14.4	high	15.5	main	11.4
extremely	20.2	hijacker(s)	4.6	make a loss	11.6
facilities	17.2	hire	10.2	manage	18.5
factory	3.4	history	8.6	map	17.4

WORDLIST

marathon	3.4	pass (a test)	3.4	reading lamp	2.5
marital status	1.2	pass an exam	14.4	reception	12.2
marriage	3.1	passport	13.3	record	14.2
mask	8.6	pasta	5.5	recruits	6.2
match	20.4	peaceful	17.7	recycled	9.2
matches	19.7	pension(er)	18.1	referee	19.5
material	12.4	percussionist	14.2	refreshing	15.6
maths	14.4	perfect(ly)	14.2	regret	10.2
meaning	6.4	personal	1.2	regularly	5.2
measured	15.5	personalities	15.1	relationship	1.6
method	13.1	personality	1.2	released	4.4
middle aged	18.1	persuaded	11.4	remember	8.5
millions	8.5	pet	20.1	residents	16.2
mix with	20.5	philosopher	2.4	retired	4.2
model	6.6	philosophy	4.2	rice	5.1
modern	2.2	photo	1.5	riding	17.2
more/most famous	15.2	pick up	20.4	river trip	17.4
mosque	13.2	pick	16.6	riverside	17.4
mountainous	13.4	pickpocket(s)	4.6	robots	16.4
mountains	17.2	pieces	19.4	rocks	20.3
multiple birth	15.5	piranha (fish)	20.2	romantic	12.2
murder (v)	4.4	plan	2.5	rubbery	20.4
murder (n)	10.2	plant	16.6	rubbish	9.3
music	14.5	plastic	9.2	rugs	2.4
musician	14.2	platform	2.4	rules	19.2
nationality	1.2	play (er)	19.2	run (a business)	11.5
nephew	2.6	poisonous	20.2	sailing	17.2
niece	2.6	politics	4.2	salary	6.7
night club	5.6	pop music	1.5	salt water	16.6
noise	9.1	possible	16.3	sand	17.7
noisier	15.4	potatoes	5.5	satellites	16.6
normal	15.2	pottery	10.6	scenery	17.2
notes	13.6	power	9.6	science	4.2
nun	15.2	predictions	16.5	scientists	17.4
nurse	18.2	preparations	3.2	scuba diving	17.2
nursing	18.2	presents	12.1	seat	18.5
OAP	18.7	pretended	15.4	sex	1.2
obedient	20.5	previous	11.4	shark	20.3
object	13.1	prison	4.4	shoot off	20.4
occupation	1.2	private	15.4	shopping precinct	16.2
octopus	20.4	prize	11.2	short	15.5
offices	16.2	problems	14.4	short time	7.2
old-fashioned	4.4	professional	5.5	shuffle	19.6
open-minded	6.2	profit	11.2	sick	18.2
optional	17.7	project	11.2	sights	17.7
orchestra	14.2	properly	15.4	sightseeing	10.6
orders	11.2	protesting	4.4	signs	7.2
organise	9.5	public transport	9.2	simple	7.5
other side	19.4	punishment	4.4	situated	17.2
outdoors	6.2	punk	15.2	size	20.5
overweight	5.2	purr	20.3	small ads	1.5
pack	16.6	pushchairs	15.2	smelly/smelliest	20.2
packet	5.2	put on	9.2	snake	20.3
pale	4.4	qualifications	6.4	sofa	2.4
parachuting	10.6	quick-thinking	4.1	solar energy	16.4
parade	15.2	quiet	15.2	solution	4.4
paradise	12.2	radiators	2.5	solved	4.2
park	17.2	rafting	17.4	sound	7.5
parrot	20.3	raised platforms	16.6	special	15.4
partner	11.1	raw	5.5	spider	17.6

WORDLIST

spokesman	16.2	thinking about	6.6	veil	4.4
sport	9.5	threw	8.2	venture	11.5
spots	5.1	throat	4.4	vibrations	14.2
spray	9.6	tied	8.2	video	12.2
spring	6.6	ties	11.2	villages	17.2
spy	4.2	tiny	2.2	visa	13.2
square	19.4	toast	5.5	waist	19.5
squash	1.5	toddler	18.1	waiting	6.6
staff	6.7	together	15.4	walking stick	8.4
stamina	20.5	tomb	8.6	want(s)	3.2
standard	10.2	top	19.4	washbasin	17.6
stare (at)	15.2	tour guide	6.4	washing machine	8.5
starred	14.5	tour	10.6	waste	9.1
steak	5.5	town	15.2	water skiing	17.2
storey	16.2	traditions	12.1	water vapour	16.6
strange	14.4	traffic	9.1	waterfalls	17.2
strangers	1.1	train	20.5	wedding	12.1
strangle	4.4	training	6.2	weighed	15.5
study	3.1	tramp	8.4	whisky vat	2.4
style	8.1	translation	7.2	widow	18.7
success	11.1	transport	8.6	widower	18.7
sugar	5.2	trapeze artist	8.2	win	19.6
summer	6.6	travel	1.2	windmill	2.1
surname	1.2	traveller	13.1	windsurfing	17.2
surroundings	20.4	trekking	17.7	winner	19.6
swimming	6.6	twenties	8.1	work out	11.2
switch off	9.2	twins	15.1	work	3.1
symbols	7.2	uncrowded	17.7	working from home	16.4
system	7.2	understand	7.5	world	15.2
take-away	5.2	universal language	7.2	writing	9.2
talent	14.1	unleaded petrol	9.2	yoghurt	5.5
tasty	15.6	unpolluted	17.2	youngish	18.1
team	11.2	unusual	15.5	youth hostel	13.2
teenager	5.2	valleys	17.2	zebra	20.2
temperament	20.5	vandalism	4.6	zoo	20.1
tennis	17.2	vegetable farm	16.6	zoo-keeper	6.4
tents	17.4	vegetables	5.2	zorilla	20.2
the length of	3.2	vegetarian	5.1		

Acknowledgements

The publishers are grateful to the following for permission to reproduce the copyright material on the pages indicated.

Four facts from *The Guinness Book of Records* (p. 30), Copyright © **Guinness Publishing Ltd 1989**, letter adapted from extract from *Traveller's Tales* by Eric Newby (p 26), **HarperCollins Publishers Ltd**; text adapted from article 'Picture perfect' by Bob Pool (p 13), **Los Angeles Times Syndicate**, texts adapted from articles 'Quickstep Across Africa' by Pearson Phillips (p 5) and 'Put Two and Two Together' by Rodney Tyler (p 29), **Mail on Sunday/You Magazine**; text based on 'A Room of My Own' featuring Roger Doudna (p 4), **Observer**; text on Operation Raleigh (p 6), **Operation Raleigh**; text based on article 'Architecture, Japanese City of the Future' (p 31), **Joanna Pitman**; information on Weddings in Paradise (p 23), **Worldwide Thomson**.

Teacher's Book: definition from *Collins COBUILD English Language Dictionary* (p 27), © **HarperCollins Publishers Ltd**.

Photographs

J Allen Cash Ltd (p 33); All-Sport (U.K.) Ltd (p 2); Aspect Picture Library Ltd (p 21); BBC Photographic Library (p 7); Bridgeman Arts Library Ltd (p 15); Camera Press Ltd (p 36); C.O.I (p 11); Cephas Picture Library (p 35); The Cinema Museum (p 7); Bruce Coleman Ltd (p 17); Colorific/Telegraphic Colour Library (pp 24, 29); Colorsport (p 27); Terry Cryer (p 11); Flora Duff-Torrance (p 33); E.T. Archive (p 27); Eric Ellington (p 4); Greg Evans International (Photo Library) (p 25); Mary Evans Picture Library (p 15); Sally and Richard Greenhill (pp 1, 2, 11, 35); Susan Griggs Agency Ltd (pp 1, 2, 21, 23, 28); Robert Harding Picture Library Ltd (pp 3, 11, 16); The Hu Hon Picture Company (p 15); The Hutchinson Library (p 23); The Image Bank (pp 3, 21, 33, 34); Images Colour Library (p 23); International Stock Exchange Photo Library (pp 1, 21); The Kobal Collection Ltd (p 27); The Mansell Collection (p 15); NHPA (p 17); Network Photographers (p 1); Orpix (p 2); Popperfoto (p 16); Rex Features Ltd (pp 23, 28); Tony Stone Worldwide Photo Library (pp 3, 17, 23, 35); Universal Pictorial Press and Agency Ltd (p 28); The Vintage Magazine Co Ltd (p 16); World Pictures (p 25)
All other photos by Sue Baker

Picture research by Mandy Twells

Illustrations

Paul Bateman (pp 13, 31); Ken Binder – Satchel Illustrators (pp 9/10, 37); Christina Brimage (pp 15/16, 21, 27/28, 29, 35); David Brindley (pp 7/8); Richard Draper (ppT14, 32, 57); Angelica Elsebach (pp 39/40); Antonia Enthoven (pp 4, 18, 22, 30, 36); Sue Hillwood-Harris (pp 5/6); Tania Hurt-Newton (pp 12, 22, 27, 32, 34, 40, 41, 43, 47, 51); Jo Lawrence (pp 19/20); Joanna Quinn (pp 48, 49, 55, 60); Tracy Ramsdale (p 18); Sue Shields (p 4); Emma Sutherland (pp 25/26); all airbrush work by John Gilkes.

The publishers have made every effort to contact owners of copyright. Thy apologise for any omissions, and if details are sent, will be glad to rectify these when the title is reprinted.

Teacher's Book Project artwork: Mary Walsh

Design: Shireen Nathoo